Praise for *ReThink Your Life*

"Stan Toler is a gifted and prolific author. He is a living example of the principles he teaches in *ReThink Your Life*. These principles have served him well, and you will be well served to adapt them for your own 'total quality life.'"

Dr. Thomas H. Hermiz
General Superintendent
Churches of Christ in Christian Union

"God desires for us to live in total freedom in Christ. Unfortunately we can become chained by our destructive and unhealthy thoughts. *ReThink Your Life* takes you on a powerful spiritual journey to understand the importance and practical ways to renew your mind and live victoriously!"

Craig Groeschel
Senior Pastor
LifeChurch.tv

"This prescription for maintaining a healthy Christ-centered mind is powerful. You must read this volume."

Doug M. Carter
Senior Vice President of EQUIP

"Stan Toler has done it again! He has contributed a very practical book on the Christian life to help people know God better and serve him more effectively. This may be Stan's greatest contribution yet."

Elmer L. Towns
Dean, School of Religion
Liberty University

"Timely, impacting, relevant! *ReThink Your Life* will enable readers to 'bring all our thoughts into subjection to the mind of Christ.' Start this diet today!"

Bob R. Ely
President, Southwestern Christian University

"This volume is power packed with tools to finally correct one of the most neglected areas in our development as believers. I highly recommend it as a valuable commodity to anyone who is committed to discovering their purpose, renewing their minds and truly becoming transformed believers for God!"

Dr. M. L. Jemison
Senior Pastor
St. John Missionary Baptist Church

"*ReThink Your Life* gives practical, scripturally based guidance to improving our thought processes. I heartily endorse this book for anyone seeking to enhance and empower their lives by recognizing and doing something positive about personal destructive or non-productive behaviors."

Raymond F. Culpepper
Presiding Bishop
Church of God (Cleveland, Tenn.)

"*ReThink Your Life* is a brilliant concept, superbly written."

Debra White Smith
Best-Selling Author and Speaker

"Stan Toler provides a practical approach for us to take inventory of our lives and reassess our priorities; and provides us with a practical plan to accomplish that . . . Stan's inner desire and personal commitment to help people achieve *Total Quality Life* is evident throughout the pages of this book."

Lane Roberds
Director of Training and Development
B. C. Clark Inc., Jewelers

"Stan is the master of practical, challenging us to intentionally exchange our poor mental diet for a healthy intake in light of our screen-fixated society."

Ron Hunter Jr.
Executive Director and CEO
Randall House Publishers

ReThink
YOUR Life

A Unique
Diet to Renew
Your Mind

ReThink
YOUR Life

STAN TOLER

Compliments of…

wesleyan publishing house
P.O. Box 50434
Indianapolis, IN 46250-0434

Call: 800.493.7539 • Fax: 800.788.3535
E-mail: wph@wesleyan.org • Online: www.wesleyan.org/wph

Please send copies of any review or mention.

wesleyan
publishing
house

Indianapolis, Indiana

Copyright © 2008 by Stan Toler
Published by Wesleyan Publishing House
Indianapolis, Indiana 46250
Printed in the United States of America
ISBN: 978-0-89827-373-1

Library of Congress Cataloging-in-Publication Data

Toler, Stan.
  Rethink your life : a unique diet to renew your mind / Stan Toler.
      p. cm.
  Includes bibliographical references and index.
  ISBN 978-0-89827-373-1 (alk. paper)
  1. Thought and thinking--Religious aspects--Christianity. 2.
Christianity and culture. 3. Spiritual life--Christianity. I. Title.
  BV4598.4.T65 2008
  248.4--dc22
                              2008012014

To President John Fozard of Mid-America Christian University—
Your leadership and passion to educate and stretch
the minds of young leaders inspire me.

Contents

ACKNOWLEDGMENTS

Many thanks to Donald D. Cady, Lawrence W. Wilson,
Joe Jackson, Lyn Rayn, and the entire team at
Wesleyan Publishing House for their faith in this project.
Thanks also to Jerry Brecheisen, Delores Leonard,
Adam Palmer, Jeff Dunn, Tom Winters, Mary McNeil,
and Pat Diamond for their invaluable assistance.

Introduction

C ogito ergo sum."

This is Latin. Don't worry, it's the only Latin in this book, and now it's behind you.

What does it mean? It's a translation of the well-known French quotation "Je pense, donc je suis."

You might know it better as "I think, therefore I am."

Perhaps your reaction to the phrase is something like, "Duh! Of course." But when René Descartes first published the thought in 1637, it was groundbreaking. People had been using their minds (more or less) since God breathed life into Adam, but rarely had they thought about the mind itself or how it functions. Descartes's statement was a turning point for people's awareness of their thought processes, and it became a hinge of modern philosophy.

Unfortunately, too few people today think about their own thought processes much less taking steps to improve them. Yet the mind left untended becomes a fertile breeding ground for all kinds of destructive or unproductive thinking which almost always results in destructive or unproductive behavior.

As I said in my book *Total Quality Life*, "Thoughts become attitudes. Attitudes become actions. Actions become habits. Therefore, the key to controlling your life is to control your mind."[1] In order to live happy, healthy, productive lives—total quality lives—people must care for their minds. The good news is, despite what you might be thinking right now, you can do it! That's what *ReThink Your Life* is all about—caring for our minds, so that we're empowered to experience total quality life.

MY PERSONAL JOURNEY

My journey with this mind renewal diet began at the prompting of Dr. Melvin Maxwell, my college president, who took his now famous son, John C. Maxwell, and me to the Positive Mental Attitude rallies in Dayton, Ohio. The speakers' inspiring messages still ring in my mind daily. I can hear W. Clements Stone saying, "What the mind can conceive, you can achieve." I needed all the help I could get with Positive Mental Attitude since I spent the early part of my childhood in a coal-mining community called

Baileysville, located in the majestic hills of West Virginia. It was a small town with a population of less than a hundred and a main street that was less of a street and more of a cul-de-sac. It featured a marvelous view of the hills, as well as an old-fashioned swinging bridge over which we could cross the river. It was the very definition of rural and, because of that, it was a place that was long on familial love though quite short on luxurious amenities.

I lived in a small, three-room house on the side of Baileysville Mountain with my mother, my father, and my two brothers, Mark and Terry. We got our water for free from a nearby well, and we kept warm in the winters with the help of our hard-working pot-bellied stove, which ran on the same coal my father mined. We didn't have a bathroom; instead, we had a well-worn path to the outhouse. It wasn't much. But it was home and we liked it.

On Saturday mornings, my family made for the Wyoming Company Store to buy supplies for the coming week. While my parents stretched their money as far as they could, my brothers and I took our weekly fill of television viewing on the black and white TV sets in the store's furniture section. We had no television at home, so this was the only way we could keep up with the adventures of Sky King. As you might imagine, we always took advantage of that crucial opportunity.

Our Saturday morning excursion was always the highlight of my week. That made it all the more tragic the time we came home from it to find our little three-room home completely engulfed in flames. Sure, we could've run to the well and started hauling water to fight the fire, but it would've been only a token effort. The house was too far gone, and it was soon a smoldering pile of ashes.

I'll never forget how my dad put his arm around Pastor Grindstaff that day and quoted a paraphrase of Job 1:21: "The LORD giveth and the LORD taketh away. Blessed be the name of the LORD." My father's faith in the face of such hardships helped provide a firm foundation for my life's work today. His profoundly positive attitude, keeping a faithful perspective even in the midst of tragedy, was a testament to his singular focus on God. I cried for days afterward, but my father never wavered in his trust that God would take care of us. Looking back, it's clear that he had a healthy mind.

He did not, however, have a healthy body. Toiling the coal mines day after day took its toll on him, and by the age of thirty-one, he'd broken his back three times down in the mines and had begun to show symptoms of black lung, the dreadful disease often contracted by coal miners.

So we packed up and moved to Columbus, Ohio, in hopes of leaving the hardscrabble life of coal mining behind us. Dad began to work in construction, and though the pay wasn't great, it kept us in pinto beans, cornbread, and fried bologna, which we had for supper nearly every night.

Then Dad got laid off in the winter of 1961. It was a tough winter that year, a winter filled with snow and frigid temperatures, but the severe climate was far from the worst of our worries. With money tight, my parents closed off the majority of the house to try to limit our utility bills.

Food was starting to become scarce too. On Christmas Eve, Mom looked in the cupboards and found no food for Christmas Day—not even our customary pinto beans, cornbread, and bologna. There was no food in the house and, with Dad out of work, no conceivable way of buying any.

Reluctantly, my family headed downtown to inquire about receiving government assistance. We parked our old Plymouth and got in line with hundreds of people all hoping that the city of Columbus could provide cheese, flour, dried milk, and powdered eggs. But even the prospect of receiving much-needed food couldn't warm our hearts enough to fend off the stinging cold along with the biting wind and blowing snow.

Finally, my father wouldn't stand for it another moment. "We're going home boys," he announced. "God will provide!" I didn't understand where his faith came from or why God wouldn't provide for us through the government assistance program, but I trusted his faith, and so did my brothers and Mom.

Once we got home, we found some popcorn in the cupboard, so that became our dinner. We boys spent the rest of the evening opening our Christmas presents, one to each of us, purchased with trading stamps from our neighborhood Top Value catalog store. After opening our presents, we gathered in our parents' bedroom for the night, our stomachs full of popcorn, our hearts full of familial love, and our minds full of anxiety about tomorrow's nonexistent breakfast menu.

The next morning, my tight-knit family was awakened by a loud knock at the front door and the muffled shout of "Merry Christmas!" We rushed to the door, threw it open, and found a crowd of people from our church, Fifth Avenue Church, standing on our doorstep with Christmas gifts, clothes, and, most importantly, a month's worth of food— including our beloved pinto beans, cornmeal, and bologna. Merry Christmas, indeed!

GOD IS STILL IN HEAVEN

In a way, my dad's expression of faith in desperate circumstances was like that of King Jehoshaphat. Facing an escalating military threat from three nations—Moab, Ammon, and Mount Seir—Jehoshaphat knew his tiny kingdom of Judah couldn't defeat these enemies. Not on its own, anyway.

So he turned to God, seeking the Lord's assistance in front of an assembled throng of the entire nation:

O LORD, God of our fathers, are you not the God who is in heaven? You rule over all the kingdoms of the nations. Power and might are in your hand, and no one can withstand you. O our God, did you not drive out the inhabitants of this land before your people Israel and give it forever to the descendants of Abraham your friend? They have lived in it and have built in it a sanctuary for your Name, saying, "If calamity comes upon us, whether the sword of judgment, or plague or famine, we will stand in your presence before this temple that bears your Name and will cry out to you in our distress, and you will hear us and save us" (2 Chron. 20:6–9).

Notice how Jehoshaphat begins his prayer with the rhetorical question "Are you not the God who is in heaven?" Jehoshaphat is reminding himself—and the assembled mass of Judeans—that *of course* God can do anything. He's "the God who is in heaven" for crying out loud! These seemingly invincible enemies from Ammon, Moab, and Mount Seir are of no consequence compared to God. By asking the question, Jehoshaphat is attempting to refocus the minds and hearts of his people onto what really counts— God's sovereignty and might.

In the next verse, Jehoshaphat continues with more rhetorical questions: "O our God, did you not drive out the inhabitants of this land before your people Israel and give it forever to the descendants of Abraham your friend?" While the first question reminded God's people of God's power, the second galvanized their hearts and minds, including Jehoshaphat himself, by focusing on God's faithfulness. God not only possesses the power to act, he has a history of using that power to act on behalf of his people. What a healthy way to think in the midst of adversity!

Now I can see that my dad thought the same way about God as Jehoshaphat did. Standing in line on Christmas Eve, my father as much as lifted his eyes and cried out, "Are you not the God of the heavens? Have you not provided for us in the past?" My dad had such a strong faith in God's provision that he knew he could trust God to take complete care of us.

Though my father passed away less than a year later in an accident, his faith remains with me to this day, as an example and an inspiration. While I recognize that I enjoyed some advantages that many others haven't, such as growing up in a faithfull family, my hardships, including the loss of my father, were very real too. The bitter aspects of my experience could have easily compelled me to a life of self-pity and aimlessness. Instead, by God's grace and because of my father's example, my childhood instilled in me a desire to help people lead a total quality life.

THE REASON FOR THIS BOOK

You too can have faith like my father and King Jehoshaphat—faith that will carry you through whatever the circumstance. You can learn to function well in all facets of your life and enjoy a healthy spiritual life, healthy emotional life, healthy financial life, healthy relational life—the list goes on. But one key prerequisite to all these different types of health is having a healthy mind. If you're struggling with a particular area in your life, it's quite likely that your thinking about that area is not as healthy as it could be. You may need to "be transformed by the renewing of your mind" (Rom. 12:2). It might be time for you to go on a mind renewal diet.

Thus, my motivation to write this book. My heart's passion is to help you live a total quality life, to help you make the most of your all-too-brief time on this earth. And if you aren't functioning well, if you aren't making the most of your life, I propose that you focus on developing a healthier mind. I know there are times when my mind is not as healthy as it should be. Even now, I sometimes allow negative and destructive ideas to creep into my thinking. It requires awareness, discipline, and the power of the Holy Spirit to restore my mind back to health. That's where this unique diet can be of great help to you.

HOW TO USE THIS BOOK

This book will teach you a four-phase process for restoring order and cleanliness to your thought life. The four phases are:

> Detoxification
>
> Realignment
>
> Reinforcement
>
> Perseverance

Each of the first three phases can be completed in one week, so that you can work through the bulk of your mind renewal diet in about three weeks. But the results you achieve can last forever!

The fourth phase, Perseverance, focuses on the transition from diet to lifestyle. In it you'll learn to challenge your mind so that you experience all the benefits of being a lifelong learner. In a sense, this fourth week stretches into a lifetime as you make healthy thinking a way of life.

Each week of your mind renewal diet, you'll learn new behaviors you can incorporate into your life to promote healthy thinking. These are not so much steps to healthy thinking, as if you leave one behind and move up to the next higher step, but practices of healthy living that you can gradually layer on top of one another. Learning them one at a time over a three-week time frame is much simpler and easier than trying to incorporate them all in a single day.

At the end of each chapter, you'll find a Lock It Down section that offers five practical actions you can take to apply the new behavior you've learned in that chapter to your own life. Don't feel as if you need to complete every action in the Lock It Down section for one practice before moving on to the next practice. It's okay to skip some actions and come back to them later. However, do choose at least one or two actions to work with right away before moving on. That's the only way that you'll move beyond reading about change to actually making a change. Also, resist the temptation to always look through and find the ones that seem easiest to you. It's okay to do that every now and then, but most of the time, challenge yourself to do one of the actions that requires more effort. You'll get much more benefit from the mind renewal process that way. As you try various actions and decide which ones work best for you, you'll be building a system for renewing your mind that God can use to make an incredible difference in the way that you think, feel, and act.

I'm not going to tell you it's easy to bring about change in your way of thinking, but it is doable! And it's essential for anyone who wants to live a well-ordered, productive life. With this mind renewal diet as your guide and with the Holy Spirit empowering your transformation, you'll be surprised at how quickly you begin to see a major difference in the way you think and act.

Once you've finished reading *ReThink Your Life*, return to it often. My hope is that this will not be a book that you read once and then store on a shelf. Keep this book handy and use it! Refer to it often so that the process of renewing your mind sinks below the surface and becomes a way of life for you. Review the principles again. Try exercises you might have skipped the first time. And continue to experience victory, through God's power, in the battle for your mind.

VICTORY IS WITHIN REACH

Renewing the mind is an ongoing battle. Satan and his slaves will not give up the battle to enslave your mind until Jesus returns. But—and here's the key—you can have victory today. You can have victory tomorrow and the next day. This mind renewal diet is your battle plan; it will lead you to victory in the daily war for your mind. And as one small victory leads to a series of victories, and a series of victories leads to a victorious lifestyle, you'll soon be able to look back and see how God has used this mind renewal process to change the way you think. It can have a positive impact on every area of your life.

I hope and pray that, as we embark on this journey together, you will take these lessons to heart—and to mind. It is my sincere dream that every person in this world, in the complete spectrum of existence, would cherish every breath of air as a gift from God, because that is exactly what they are.

Phase 1

DETOXIFICATION

WEEK ONE

Practice 1

Surrender Control

FOCUS

to gain control

of your mind,

relinquish control

of your life

S o, wait. The first step to winning the battle for my mind is to surrender? Absolutely. You got it. Okay, let me explain. Think of the Christian life, as the Bible so often describes it, in terms of warfare. There is a huge difference between supporting a war verbally and actually stepping onto a battlefield. It's pretty easy to sit in the comfort of your living room, watching debates in congress or listening to news pundits, and decide whether you are for or against a particular military action. In our day, supporting a war doesn't necessarily require us to reorder our lives or make any sacrifice whatsoever. In many cases, people can talk at length about why they are for or against a war and then go on about life completely unaffected. It's not as if they're volunteering to be the first one into the firefight.

Not so with a soldier. Enlisted men and women surrender their very lives in support of a country's defense or other military objectives. Soldiers relinquish much of their time, comfort, convenience, desires, freedom, and safety to serve the country and its mission. They place themselves under the command of their country's leaders, agreeing to go where they are commanded to go and do what they are commanded to do in the way they are commanded to do it. While they can only trust that their leaders are concerned for their safety and well-being, they expect their leaders to always act in the best interests of their country. They agree to participate in whatever military action their leaders deem necessary to protect the nation's welfare, no matter the cost. For a person who enlists, supporting a war means nothing short of total and complete surrender.

Many professing Christians approach their faith more as couch potatoes, arm-chair commentating about the war, than as soldiers stepping onto the battlefield. They verbally support the concept of building Jesus' kingdom, but they stop short of volunteering for service or even inconveniencing themselves for the sake of the mission. They fail to relinquish control of their time, their goals, and their desires to the supreme Commander-in-Chief. They never quite make it, in a sense, to the recruiter's office, to the point of surrendering their lives, their hearts, and their minds to the service of Christ.

But the call to faith in Jesus is not a call to a sedentary lifestyle of comfort and indulgence. It is a call to an active life of service,

BRAIN FACTS

Number of neurons in the brain (average): 100 billion

Number of neocortical neurons lost each day: 85,000

The good news: The brain continues to produce new neurons throughout our lives, and it does so in response to stimulation (exercise). This is referred to as *brain plasticity.*

to participate in God's plan to rescue and transform the world. To live such a life, we must first surrender our minds to be transformed, so that we can begin to think, as much as possible, the way Jesus thought. The good news is that we don't have to accomplish all this in our own power. Instead God gave us his Spirit who transforms and empowers us to live the life God calls us to and to think the way Jesus thinks.

Perhaps you've never before considered that Jesus desires and expects to be lord of the way you think. In fact, the Bible has quite a lot to say about our minds.

MIND BY DESIGN

God designed and gave us our minds—a unique gift to the pinnacle of his creation—and with them, instructions for their care and use laid out in black and white in his Word. Here is a small sampling, with my emphasis added:

- "Love the Lord your God with all your heart and with all your soul and with all your *mind*" (Matt. 22:37).

- "Love the Lord your God with all your heart and with all your soul and with all your *mind* and with all your strength" (Mark 12:30).

- "Love the Lord your God with all your heart and with all your soul and with all your strength and with all your *mind*" (Luke 10:27).

- "Then he opened their *minds* so they could understand the Scriptures" (Luke 24:45).

- "Those who live according to the sinful nature have their *minds* set on what that nature desires; but those who live in accordance with the Spirit have their *minds* set on what the Spirit desires" (Rom. 8:5).

- "Do not conform any longer to the pattern of this world, but be transformed by the renewing of your *mind*" (Rom. 12:2).

- "Whatever is true, whatever is noble, whatever is right, whatever is pure, whatever is lovely, whatever is admirable— if anything is excellent or praiseworthy—*think* about such things" (Phil. 4:8).

As you can see, our minds are on God's mind quite a bit. Maybe we need to pay more attention to our minds too.

LORD OF THE WAY WE THINK

As Christians, we are to surrender our minds so that Jesus becomes lord of the way we think. Now, surrendering our minds doesn't mean that we stop thinking. Not at all. Christians can and should be among the most logical, rational, intellectually curious people in the world. Remember that God created our minds, and he expects us to use them to the best of our abilities!

Nor does it mean that we should uncritically accept any idea or thought that presents itself as Christian. There are lots of people out there claiming to be Christian teachers whose ideas, attitudes, and practices don't measure up to Scripture. And some of what is simply accepted in our culture as a Christian point of view is inconsistent with, or opposed to, the teachings of Jesus. The Bible teaches Christians to "test everything. Hold on to the good" (1 Thess. 5:21).

"A Mind Is a Terrible Thing to Waste" has been the fund-raising slogan of the United Negro College Fund for more than thirty-five years, and has made its way into the American vernacular.

Surrendering your mind to Christ *does* mean to choose Jesus as your mentor or teacher, to trust his wisdom as a guide for your life. It means to trust that his way of understanding and making sense of the world is true, accurate, and sufficient. If you choose to believe what Jesus believes, to order your life according to the principles he teaches, and to offer your life in his service, then you are surrendering your mind to Jesus.

Learning to think the way Jesus thinks doesn't happen in an evening or a weekend. Just as soldiers go through basic training to prepare themselves for military service, Christians must submit themselves to training for Kingdom service. The mind renewal diet will help you train your mind to participate effectively in service to your King. Instead of being easily persuaded and blown about by every thought or idea that floats through your mind, you'll learn to proactively select and act on the thoughts and behaviors that strengthen your life in Christ.

Memory is a function of the mind, and there are two types of memories: *explicit* memories, which are facts and events; and *implicit* memories, which remind you how to do something. For example, the answers to the questions on a history test are (hopefully!) explicit memories. Implicit memories remind you how to actually write the responses.

MIND ASSAULT

Just as soldiers guard themselves against those who might attack their positions, the soldier of Christ will guard against assaults on the mind, whether the attacks are out in the open or more insidious. They understand, as C. S. Lewis wrote in *Mere*

Christianity, that every decision they make affects their ability to guard their mind and thinking:

> Every time you make a choice you are turning the central part of you, the part of you that chooses, into something a little different from what it was before. And taking your life as a whole, with all your innumerable choices, all your life long you are slowly turning this central thing either into a heavenly creature or into a hellish creature; either into a creature that is in harmony with God, and with other creatures, and with itself, or else into one that is in a state of war and hatred with God, and with its fellow creatures, and with itself.[1]

The empires of the future are the empires of the mind.
—Sir Winston Churchill

What we think about is what we become. Unfortunately, many of us disregard this truth and carelessly ingest unhealthy content into our minds that inevitably produces a myriad of unhealthy thoughts, attitudes, and eventually, behaviors.

For example, even though we know we aren't what we drive, we've allowed marketers and advertisers into our homes and into our minds, and they have convinced us otherwise. How many people do you know (perhaps you're one of them) who are driving cars they can't afford because of the way it makes them feel or look? They've exchanged financial health for an image of prosperity.

Here's another one. What's the best and healthiest way to lose weight? Eat less (and better) and exercise more, right? Of course. Yet the diet industry raked in about fifty-five billion dollars in 2006 and is expected to exceed sixty billion dollars in 2008.[2] Even though we know what it takes to lose weight, we let the advertising industry convince us that the newest pill or the next plan will be the magic bullet we've been waiting for. We exchange common-sense living for untested, unproven methodologies, many of which may end up causing more harm than good.

So how do we move from unconsciously accepting and acting on whatever thoughts or ideas bombard our minds to proactively choosing what we will believe and how we will act? We put ourselves on a thought diet.

MIND FUEL

The plain fact of the matter is that your mind, just like an automobile, needs fuel to operate. Fill your car with higher-quality gasoline and it'll run better. In the same way, your mind will function better when you fill it with premium fuel. And when it comes to your mind, I can guarantee that you'll be able to afford the better stuff.

Or, compare it to your body. Remember when you were in elementary school and you learned about the food pyramid that provides a guide for healthy eating? You may have learned four major food groups, or you may have learned five. Now the USDA says there are six! They are: grains, vegetables, fruits, oils, milk, and meat and beans.[3]

God designed our bodies to rely on healthy portions of a variety of foods. We were never meant to exist on a strict diet of Big Macs and french fries. Not that there's anything wrong with those things intrinsically—they're fine every once in a while. If all you eat is junk food, however, you're going to wind up with a junky body.

Astonishingly, your mind operates on the same principle as your body. What goes in is what's going to come out. Our minds are bombarded by so much junk—some of it unavoidable, some of it we welcome—that they get cluttered and overwhelmed, and our thoughts become cloudy and distorted. What's worse than having a junky body? Having a junky mind!

In order to have healthy minds, we must have healthy thoughts. Just as the health of our bodies depends, in part, on the content of the foods we consume, the fitness of our minds correlates with the healthiness of the ideas we embrace.

But how can we know the difference between healthy and unhealthy thoughts? What sort of thoughts are on our approved mind food pyramid? Remember the passage I quoted above, Philippians 4:8: "Whatever is true, whatever is noble, whatever is right, whatever is pure, whatever is lovely, whatever is admirable—if anything is excellent or praiseworthy—think about such things." There are your healthy mind food groups.

Of course Philippians 4:8 is easily quoted, but not as easily practiced. Our minds tend to be so crowded, it's a challenge to search for and destroy all the thoughts that fail to meet the Philippians 4:8 standard, and even more difficult to prevent them from entering our minds in the first place. The key, again, to gaining control of your mind is to first surrender control of your mind, heart, and body, to give it over to your supreme Commander-in-Chief, Jesus. More about that after an important introduction.

THE MIND OF THE LORD IN SCRIPTURE

"Who has understood the mind of the LORD, or instructed him as his counselor?" (Isa. 40:13; see also Rom. 11:34).

"'For who has known the mind of the Lord that he may instruct him?' But we have the mind of Christ" (1 Cor. 2:16).

MEET JAKE

As we journey together through the different practices involved in renewing your mind, you'll learn about a person I've created to journey along with us. This is not an actual person, but more a conglomeration of people, a collection of experiences with mind renewal. Let's call him Jake.

> Change is the essence of life. Be willing to surrender what you are for what you could become.
>
> —Author Unknown

Jake has a fairly good life. He has a wife whom he loves and a couple of kids who are the delight of his eyes, to borrow a biblical-sounding phrase. He isn't wealthy, but he isn't poor. He has a job that pays the bills and takes care of the mortgage, that puts food on the table for his family and allows them to take a vacation every once in a while. He buys a tall cup of coffee, with room for cream, at Starbucks every day on his way into work; he often meets his wife and kids for lunch at the pasta place down the street from his office, or, depending on how close payday is, Taco Bell.

In his spare time, Jake likes to read the occasional best-selling novel or go to the movies to catch whatever is popular at the time. He has a few favorite TV shows, including the news, which he usually catches with his wife after the kids are in bed. He watches a lot of sports and DVDs on the weekends, but not so much that it interferes with his family time. Driving, he listens to music or talk radio, and while he's at work, he mostly works, but he does enjoy the occasional e-mail forward from a friend and reading up on his favorite Web sites.

Jake and his family attend a thriving church and have many friends and acquaintances there. He sings harmony during praise and worship and takes notes during the sermon, though sometimes his mind wanders when his pastor preaches. He smiles when he shakes hands during greeting time and looks people in the eye when he talks to them.

But, and here's the catch, Jake still feels a little empty and spiritually lethargic; like he's carrying around excess weight in his soul. He believes he's a Christian, but he doesn't see much evidence of God's power transforming his life. Though he tries to read his Bible (occasionally), he doesn't really get it or have the time (he thinks) to figure it out. He's pretty sure he loves God and (most of) God's people, but he's not really serving them or others in any way that he can see. Like a person who has packed on a little too much around his middle, Jake has an overweight mind that indulges a little too much on junk food and not enough on spiritual nourishment.

What is a man like Jake to do to shake off his sluggish spirit? He needs a mind renewal diet. But, just like any other diet, a thought diet will only help if Jake makes a full commitment to it. A nutritional diet won't work if we don't commit to eating the right foods, and a mind renewal diet won't work if we don't commit to thinking the right thoughts.

What Jake—along with the rest of us—really needs is to learn how to think the right thoughts (which then produce the right behaviors) by committing his heart and mind to righteousness. Jesus made it plain in Matthew 15:19 that our hearts, when left to their own devices, are the source of ungodliness in our lives. That's why the first step of the mind renewal diet is a complete relinquishment of the mind and heart to the One who created them in the first place.

Not to say that Jake has to be perfect. Nor do you. Nor do I. That's the whole point of salvation, and living a life submitted to God—that we are imperfect people who are in need of help. Be honest with yourself; don't try to put a happy face on your bad days. If you're lonely, angry, or discouraged, admit it to yourself with honesty and then give your feelings and circumstances over to God to help you get through them. But in order to live with healthy minds, we must have healthy spiritual hearts, and to do that, we must give up ownership of our hearts. We must give that ownership to our Creator.

Taking such a step is extraordinarily countercultural. In our culture, it's almost indisputable dogma that we're entitled to do as we please as long as it doesn't infringe on someone else's rights. If it feels good, do it—that's the underlying message we receive on a near-constant basis. As the poet William Earnest

Henley taught us, we are the masters of our fate, the captains of our soul. To surrender our hearts and minds to the control of another, even our Creator, goes against the grain of nearly every message we are bombarded with in our culture. And yet, it's exactly the step that we all need to take in order to gain control of our minds, and thus our lives.

At this point in his life, Jake has seized control of his heart. He may have surrendered it to God some time ago, but he isn't allowing God to change him any longer. He has taken back the control of his heart, and it is having a negative impact on his mind. To break out of his spiritual lethargy, Jake must again relinquish control of his heart. He needs to surrender his heart to God day-by-day, hour-by-hour, minute-by-minute, inviting the Lord to infuse his heart with God's presence.

SWEET SURRENDER

In a physical diet, we need to give up control over what we eat and surrender our desires for junky food in exchange for foods that nourish our bodies. We must care for our bodies as God intended, feeding them the types of foods he designed them to consume. The same holds true for a diet to renew your mind. When we enter into a mind renewal diet, the first step is to give up control over what we think and surrender our desire for unhealthy mind food in favor of that which is pleasing to God. Unhealthy thoughts flow from the heart, which means we must also give up control of our hearts to God. If you're still clinging on to that control, you need to surrender it to the Maker of your mind, body, and heart.

How do you do that? Simply make the decision, and then invite God to transform your heart through saying a simple prayer. Even if you've prayed a prayer like this in the past, praying it again is a great way to remind yourself whose child you are, and to affirm that you want God to be in charge of your life—including your heart and mind. Ask him to change you from the inside out. Pray that God will help you relinquish control of your heart, and therefore your mind, to him. Not only is it the first step toward a healthy mind, but it's the most important thing you can ever do in your life.

- *Admit that you have sinned.* "For all have sinned and fall short of the glory of God" (Rom. 3:23).

- *Believe that Jesus Christ died for you.* "Yet to all who received him, to those who believed in his name, he gave the right to become children of God" (John 1:12).

- *Confess that Jesus Christ is Lord of your Life.* "If you confess with your mouth, 'Jesus is Lord,' and believe in your heart that God raised Him from the dead, you will be saved. For it is with your heart that you believe and are justified, and it is with your mouth that you confess and are saved" (Rom. 10:9–10).

Dear Lord Jesus, I know I am a sinner. I believe you died for my sins and arose from the grave. I now turn from my sins and invite you to come in and transform my heart and life. I receive you as my personal Savior and follow you as my Lord. Amen.

Jake got up from his knees feeling as though he was a new man. He knew God had heard his prayer, and he knew he truly wanted God to be in charge of his life again. This prayer was only a first step, but Jake was sure it was a step in the right direction.

In the Lock It Down section, you'll find a number of exercises that will help you begin to surrender your heart and mind to Jesus, as well as to prepare for the next practice in the mind renewal diet: detoxifying your mind.

LOCK IT DOWN

Now complete these five exercises to apply what you learned in this chapter.

1. As you begin this unique diet, take some time to seriously consider what you hope to accomplish through the process. Write out or journal your answers to the following questions:

What changes do you hope to see in your life? What outcomes do you expect to experience? What would make your mind renewal diet a success for you?

2. When setting goals, it's helpful to make them as specific and measurable as possible. In writing them, you can answer the question, "How will I know for sure that I've accomplished this goal?" After considering what you hope to accomplish through the mind renewal process, write out some specific, measurable goals for yourself. Later, you can use them to evaluate the difference the mind renewal diet is making in your life.

3. When we are not performing very well in a particular area in our life, most often we can trace it to an issue of knowledge, desire, or resources: I don't know enough to do well, I don't care enough to do well, or I don't have everything I need to do well. Sometimes it's a combination of two or three of the factors. Keep a private list of each of your mind struggles this week. In each case, note whether it is an issue of knowledge, desire, or resources.

4. As you go through this process, you'll learn much more about the unhealthy ideas that bombard our minds from a variety of sources. Before going on, take some time to identify what you suspect are the most common sources of

unhealthy ideas in your own life. Pray now that the Holy Spirit would help you identify those sources and empower you to experience victory over the unhealthy ideas that flow from those sources.

5. Choose one of the Bible verses in the Mind By Design section and memorize it. (You can do it!)

Practice 2

Detoxify
Your Mind

FOCUS

eliminate mental

junk food from

your daily intake

love junk food. Give me a bag of Cheetos or nacho chips and a bowl of M & M's with a Diet Coke, and I am one happy man (especially if the Oklahoma Sooners are playing football on TV).

Many diets start with a period of detoxification. Usually it's a time of abstaining from junk food or other kinds of unhealthy eating habits. It can also be a time of cleansing, of consuming more of the right kinds of foods, especially those that clean up your digestive system. The idea is that you can start over again with a completely healthy foundation.

In the same way, the second layer of the mind renewal diet is detoxifying your mind, purifying it, cleansing it from the junk that so easily accumulates because of our culture and our own thoughts. It isn't easy, but it's essential for success in letting Jesus master your mind. And with a little guidance, effort, and help from the Holy Spirit, you'll put this practice in place, no problem.

WHY DETOXIFY?

There are two reasons why detoxification is sometimes necessary and helpful. One is the sheer volume of information that assaults our minds on a daily basis. While people in every age have found ways to gather information, communicate with others, and entertain themselves, never has any culture in the history of the universe been so saturated with sights and sounds as the culture that we're living in today. We're bombarded from so many angles and at such a fast rate that it is literally impossible for us to process each one and consider it separately. We simply don't know the long-term effects of such overstimulation of our senses, but there can be no doubt that it carries negative consequences in terms of our spiritual and emotional health.

Have you considered detoxing from carbonated soft drinks? Perhaps these intriguing uses for cola will persuade you.

1. Rinse dyed hair with a can of cola to lighten the color.

2. Clean corroded coins by soaking them in cola.

3. Clean tile grout with cola.

4. To get the smell out of fishing clothes, wash them in cola.

5. To remove oil stains from your driveway, pour a can of cola on the spots, let it set for a few minutes, then hose off.

6. For a green lawn and no bugs, combine a can of cola, a cup of ammonia, and $1/_4$ cup of dish soap. Spray on your yard once a month.

Why drink it when there are so many other more beneficial uses?

The other reason why detoxification is necessary is because of the unhealthy content of all those sensory messages we're receiving each day. Most of them fail to live up to the Philippians 4:8 standard. In fact, many of the messages we are constantly bombarded by are downright depressing, demeaning, or destructive. Allowed free rein, they can damage our souls. What we experience through our senses—images, words, sounds, music—stays with us for a long time, and when our senses receive unholy, damaging messages, the residual effects can be quite destructive. We need to detoxify so that the Spirit can purge us of all that lingering gunk that's stained our minds.

I find television very educating. Every time somebody turns on the set, I go into the other room and read a book.

—Groucho Marx

While it may not be possible for you to completely rid your system of every damaging thought, you can experience tremendous success in holding such thoughts captive and preventing them from negatively affecting your life.

Completely eliminating bad memories is not really a goal of the mind renewal process because it's wasted effort. All that is needed is to control and contain those negative thoughts, so that they are no longer able to harm you. As you do so, you are clearing the clutter from your mind so that positive, healthy, productive thoughts and ideas can make their way to the forefront of your mind and stay there.

FRONTAL ASSAULT

This daily attack on our minds comes from two different fronts—an external front and an internal front. The external front is our culture and the environment in which we live. Scientists in many different fields have studied the effects of such sensory overload on the brain, on behavior, and on the personality. Here are some of their findings regarding music and television, in particular.

[Repetitive music] causes a person to either enter a state of subconscious thinking or a state of anger. Dr. Michael Ballam goes on to say that "The human mind shuts down after three or four repetitions of a rhythm, or a melody, or a harmonic progression." Furthermore, excessive repetition causes people to release control of their thoughts. Rhythmic repetition is used by people who are trying to push certain ethics in their music.[1]

In 2003, Craig Anderson and Iowa State University colleague Nicholas Carnagey and Janie Eubanks of the Texas Department of Human Services reported that violent music lyrics increased aggressive thoughts and hostile feelings among five hundred college students. They concluded, "There are now good theoretical and empirical reasons to expect effects of music lyrics on aggressive behavior to be similar to the well-studied effects of exposure to TV and movie violence and the more recent research efforts on violent video games."

So what are those well-studied effects?

George Gerbner has conducted the longest running study of television violence. His seminal research suggests that heavy TV viewers tend to perceive the world in ways that are consistent with the images on TV. As viewers' perceptions of the world come to conform with the depictions they see on TV, they become more passive, more anxious, and more fearful. Gerbner calls this the "Mean World Syndrome."

Gerbner's research found that those who watch greater amounts of television are more likely to:

- overestimate their risk of being victimized by crime

- believe their neighborhoods are unsafe

- believe "fear of crime is a very serious personal problem"

- assume the crime rate is increasing, even when it is not.[2]

You probably already knew that watching violent TV programs and listening to frenetic music wasn't the best way to unwind after a tough day, but did you know that doing so could possibly make you paranoid? Well, then, what about watching a sitcom or two or even the news? Here's what happens when you watch TV according to a natural health newsletter:

The volume of information that enters our brains in one week at the beginning of the twenty-first century is more than a person received in a lifetime at the beginning of the twentieth century.

The longer a person watches television, the more easily the brain slips into alpha level, a slow, steady brain-wave pattern in which the mind is in its most receptive mode. Images and suggestions are implanted directly into the mind without viewer participation. An effective hypnosis is induced and the viewer surrenders to the unending television image stream.

Television imagery is jammed together in a steady stream of information, fracturing your attention while condensing and accelerating time. These events would not happen in ordinary life. They are technical alterations only possible within the moving-image media. Living in the rapid world of television imagery, ordinary life is dull by comparison, and often, far too slow.[3]

IM (Instant Messaging) is another potential distraction from important tasks that require uninterrupted thinking. To make real progress in creative thinking, problem solving, or other knowledge work, we need to focus on priorities and keep interruptions at a minimum. With IM, you give permission to interrupt to anyone who knows your screen name.

But perhaps slow is a good thing.

Besides TV, movies, newspapers, and Internet, let's not forget e-mail, cell phones, and text and instant messaging, all of which greatly contribute to information overload.

As people are faced with growing levels of information overload, the inability to make clear and accurate decisions can increase their stress levels.

An article in the *New Scientist* magazine claimed that exposing individuals to an information-overloaded environment resulted in lower IQ scores than exposing individuals to marijuana, although these results are contested.[4]

According to some psychologists and researchers, the "data smog" that suffocates us each day may be making us ill by interfering with our sleep, sabotaging our concentration, and undermining our immune systems. David Lewis, Ph.D., a British psychologist, calls the malady *information fatigue syndrome*.

At worst, the overload can lead to indigestion, heart problems and hypertension, Lewis's case studies of business executives suggest. In its mildest form, it sparks irritability and jeopardizes work productivity.

Lewis has found similar problems in focus groups he's conducted with other managers, financial analysts, and information workers. When inundated with data, they make more mistakes, misunderstand others, and snap at coworkers and customers. The result can be flawed conclusions and foolish decisions, causing potentially great financial loss to companies.[5]

Clearly, information overload can affect us negatively in all areas of life. This is not to say that all media is bad or that media has no redeeming value or that Christians should never consume media. In fact, some media may be necessary. Perhaps you need to peruse *The Wall Street Journal* every day because it's part of your job. Possibly you thrive on listening to teaching CDs as you head to the grocery store. Maybe you're a television critic for an entertainment magazine and therefore you have to watch every new show that hits the airwaves. When your career requires you to be heavily involved in the media, it's essential that you be aware of how media can affect you and that you take appropriate measures to guard your mind and heart.

For most people, though, as much as you like your media intake, you don't necessarily need most of what you imbibe. It may feel like you do, but just like you don't need dessert with every meal, chances are you can get by with consuming far less media than you currently do.

THE MIND UNFENCED

In addition to external sources like TV, radio, books, and the Internet, your mind also receives input from an internal source; namely your heart. While the external assault on our minds can be difficult to detect, the internal assault is even more insidious. Whenever you open the gate of your mind and set it out to pasture, what do you let it graze on? Do you allow fear about your children's safety to get the best of you? Do you keep your actions pure but let your mind lust away after some dream person? Do you worry about financial ruin, letting it consume your every waking thought?

One of the primary causes of spiritual lethargy is when we allow our minds to wander aimlessly. More often than not, our minds come to rest on thoughts or ideas that are potentially destructive. In addition to managing the external threat posed by various media, detoxifying your mind also requires corralling that part of your mind that wanders and guiding it to healthier pastures, where the Philippians 4:8 standard rules.

While it's a fairly simple procedure to limit your external sensory intake, your mental and emotional intake is much more complicated to manage. Maybe that's why so many of us just let our minds roam free wherever they seek to travel.

Unfortunately, this type of mental mileage is the greatest contributor to our spiritual lethargy, and it is therefore absolutely essential to purge during the detoxify stage of the mind renewal diet. In fact, it's so important that the Bible uses warfare-type language when discussing it in 2 Corinthians 10:3–5:

> For though we live in the world, we do not wage war as the world does. The weapons we fight with are not the weapons of the world. On the contrary, they have divine power to demolish strongholds. We demolish arguments and every pretension that sets itself up against the knowledge of God, and we take captive every thought to make it obedient to Christ.

HOLD THAT THOUGHT

There's something powerful in the idea of taking captive every thought. Who does that? It's certainly not taught on TV or the radio. Rarely do you hear anyone speak publicly about controlling your thought life.

And yet that's what the Bible instructs us to do. Why? Because our hearts are corrupt and feed wrong thinking to our minds all the time. So it is up to us, by the power of the Holy Spirit, to make sure we

The average American is exposed to about three thousand advertising messages a day, and globally corporations spend over six hundred twenty billion dollars each year to make their products seem desirable and to get us to buy them.

—Michael Brower and Warren Leon

filter the thoughts that enter our minds and to purge the negative ones that are already there.

Christians are often anxious over the fleeting thoughts that pop into their heads with no warning. They wonder how they possibly could have had such a thought. They start to feel guilty and dirty, as if the experience of the thought were itself a sin. The fact is that, in most cases, we cannot prevent a specific thought from entering our mind.

A Google search of information overload yielded over two million results.

All we can do is to manage it once it's in there. If it's a negative, sinful, destructive thought, we can clamp down on it, reject it, and eject it from our minds. If it's a positive, holy, and productive thought, we can clamp down on it, meditate on it, and apply it to our lives. Sin occurs not when we experience a fleeting thought, but when we dwell on a sinful thought rather than driving it out.

On the other hand, if you find that sinful thoughts are continually popping into your head so that a thought pattern is developing, you're probably inviting such thoughts into your life in some way or another, by the material you're reading, watching, or thinking about or by the environment that you're exposing yourself to. When this happens, it's time to guard your heart by removing the stimulus, when possible, or dealing with it through prayer and accountability (both of which are discussed later in this book).

How do we know which thoughts are appropriate for Christians and which we should eject like a virus? We find the answer once again in Philippians 4:8: "Whatever is true, whatever is noble, whatever is right, whatever is pure, whatever is lovely, whatever is admirable—if anything is excellent or praiseworthy—think about such things."

As we set about to detoxify our minds, we must set them to capture mode. If our mind begins to wander into territory beyond Philippians 4:8—regardless of why it started that direction in the first place—we can snap to attention and call it to order.

A MEDIA FAST

Now that we've learned the thought-capture method of detoxifying our minds from internal assault, how can we begin to manage our external, sensory intake? For starters, you can go on a media fast. Greatly reduce the amount of data you consume, and with the time you save, renew your focus on the Creator of your mind. Turn off the television for an extended period of time. Instead of listening to the radio in your car as you drive to work, pray (more on this later). Use the Internet sparingly, only as necessary for your job.

If you journal or keep a diary, please keep up your output, but avoid going back to reread past entries and rehash problems you've struggled with in the past. Limit your reading to the Bible and similar, uplifting Bible-related texts. Send the morning newspaper directly to the recycle bin unless you need it for your profession.

Give your iPod a break. If you feel you must listen to music, choose selections that will focus your attention on God, however you experience that musically. (Is it through standard worship music? Instrumental music? Classic symphonies?)

It isn't necessary to cut off all communication with the outside world. On the contrary, God is more interested in people than anything else—so by all means, keep up your communication with your associates; just try to keep your conversations to the point and free of fluff or idle chatter. Make your words count as you talk to people. You don't need to preach to them, and you don't need to sidestep small talk; just be wise in the things you say. If you see an opportunity to insert something of substance into the conversation, do so.

If you're feeling exceptionally motivated, consider the spiritual discipline of silence: being completely quiet—no music, no speaking, and so forth—as a way to seek God and deepen your relationship with him. Try it for a short time first (an hour? fifteen minutes?). As the Holy Spirit enables you, extend that time, and see what God may be trying to say to you.

How long should this detoxification process last? How long should you be on your media fast? Phase one of the mind renewal diet is designed to be a one week process, and so I would suggest that you consider fasting from media for at least seven days. However, there's no hard and fast guideline as to how long a media fast needs to last, nothing that applies across the board to everyone. The more wrong thinking you have in you, the more spiritually overweight you are, the longer you might want to keep fasting. Some may need no more than a week; on the other hand, some have gone as long as six weeks on this type of media fast.

Pray. Seek God's help in this area. You may find that you actually want to go longer than you'd planned. And don't worry about missing out on important news—if it's really important, those around you will fill you in.

Let's take one last look at the elements of the detoxification process before we check in with Jake to see how he's applying this step.

- Take your thoughts captive.

- Go on a media fast: no TV, Internet, radio, movies, and so forth.

- Keep reading minimal and biblical.

- Journal.

- Interact with others—God cares most about people.

- Consider silence.

JAKE'S PROGRESS

And now, Jake. Jake was skeptical about this part of the mind renewal diet, especially when he realized he wouldn't be allowed to watch sports on the weekend. He toyed with the idea of starting his detox on Monday and finishing it on Saturday morning, just in time for the day's college football schedule. But he thought better of it and decided that maybe, just maybe, since he was so dedicated to his sports viewing, that this was where he needed his detox the most.

Because Jake was so interested in sports, he thought of the two-a-days he used to do in high school on the football team. At the conclusion of every summer vacation, when the team would get back together to begin practicing for the new season, they would practice twice a day for a couple of weeks. A grueling practice in the morning, some time off for lunch and a little recuperation, then back at it in the afternoons for more practice. He subsisted mainly on water and determination.

The two-a-days were worth it, though. They only lasted for a little while, and they brought the team together and helped them condition their bodies to shake off summer's rust and get them back into game shape so they could compete on the field. He thought of this rigorous training regimen and realized he would have to take the same mentality into his detox: it was going to be tough, but it was going to be worth it in the long run.

So Jake dove off the deep end and committed to a two-week detox. He filled his wife in on his plans, and she decided to detoxify with him, just to help out and maybe to restore some right thinking to her mind as well. They began on a Monday night, and the first thing they sacrificed was the syndicated sitcom they ritually watched before going to bed. They talked instead about their children and dreamed a little bit about what life would be like when they became grandparents.

On day two, Jake worried a bit on the drive to work. He was used to listening to sports talk radio or the local Christian talk station, so he was unaccustomed to being able to hear himself think. His mind began to turn to a fearful place, unrealistically worrying that he would suddenly be dismissed from his job and subsequently cast out onto the street with his family. His heart beat faster as his imagination took over. He was almost to work before he realized what he was doing; he quickly clamped down

November 16, 2006—Sixteen-year-old student Ang Chuang Yang of Singapore, has earned a place in the record books, thanks to his fast thumbs.

Yang typed a 160-character text message in just 41.52 seconds, beating the previous record by seven-tenths of a second. Each record is set by typing a standard text chosen by Guinness World Records, the organization to which the record has been submitted. The message reads: "The razor-toothed piranhas of the genera Serrasalmus and Pygocentrus are the most ferocious freshwater fish in the world. In reality they seldom attack a human."

on those thoughts and said a prayer. He resolved to clamp down more quickly the next time. As he prayed for peace in his heart and provision for his family, the fear began to melt away and his heart rate slowed to normal.

As many as twenty billion text messages are sent each month in the United States alone.

Then he began to wonder what he should say to people at work if they asked him about the big game coming up that weekend and where he was going to watch it. Such topics were common, and he didn't want to lie about it, but he also didn't want to make a big deal out of his detox; his media fast.

Jake remembered Jesus' words in Matthew 6:16–18, and felt they applied to this initial media fast portion of his mind renewal diet:

When you fast, do not look somber as the hypocrites do, for they disfigure their faces to show men they are fasting. I tell you the truth, they have received their reward in full. But when you fast, put oil on your head and wash your face, so that it will not be obvious to men that you are fasting, but only to your Father, who is unseen; and your Father, who sees what is done in secret, will reward you.

Yes, those words applied to regular fasting of meals, but surely the spirit behind them—that a fast is essentially between the person on the fast and God—was consistent with Jake's media fast. So what should Jake say when people asked him whether he'd seen the latest show, or read something in the paper or on the Internet, or what he was planning on snacking on as he watched his favorite college team take the field that weekend?

Jake ultimately decided he didn't need to say anything. "Have you seen the latest show?" could be greeted with a simple smile and "Didn't catch it, no." "Did you read about this crazy story on the Internet?" could be handled with "No, tell me about it." "What are you going to do for the game this weekend?" was deflected with a simple "You know, I honestly don't know what my plans are for the weekend," since he didn't know those plans.

He wasn't ashamed of his media fast, of his detox, but he just wanted to keep it between him, his wife, and God. He answered everyone's questions honestly and was amazed at the amount of work he got done that day while still maintaining a good amount of face time with his coworkers. He hadn't realized how much of his work day the Internet actually consumed.

As day two stretched into days three and four, Jake found himself missing his media a little less. When he'd started his mind renewal diet, he thought he wouldn't be able to live without his talk radio or the constantly updated news on his favorite Web sites, but he found himself doing fine, and actually thriving mentally as a result. His mind was clearer, his stress level had gone down, and he was sleeping better.

And his relationship with God was skyrocketing. Cutting out all the fat allowed him to focus on his Creator with greater success. It was as if he'd been eating nothing but junk food and was therefore not hungry when it came time for the main course. But now that he had cut out all those empty mental calories, he was finding himself drawn to time with God. He craved his Bible. He began to take the long way to work so he could spend more time in prayer. It was astonishing.

When the weekend came, he threw himself into his family and, instead of checking out the game, took them all to the zoo. The kids had fun, and so did he. He overheard the final score as a zoo patron checked it on his cell phone, and, amazingly, that satisfied him. Simply hearing that his favorite team had won the game was enough.

The following week followed suit. Jake found his mind clear and clean as his detox progressed. That weekend, he actually forgot about a Saturday game until he saw the final score above the fold of a newspaper in a machine as he took the family out for a pre-church breakfast the next morning.

When the time came for his media fast to conclude, Jake remembered with fondness his time in detox and, though it had been hard at times, he felt as though he might like to continue with it. He felt empowered, knowing he had taken his thoughts and his media input captive. He made a mental commitment to keeping his media intake to a minimum.

His interior thought life had also changed. He had always struggled with lust, with noticing women other than his wife and allowing a few fleeting admiring glances at them. Now that he had begun to take his thoughts captive, he had begun to notice a different slant to those thoughts. When he saw a beautiful woman, he thanked God for filling the world with beauty and reminded himself that the woman was a person to be respected, that she was someone's wife, daughter, or mother. When he saw a woman dressed enticingly, instead of salivating over her, he felt sad for her, that she felt she had to validate herself that way. He prayed that God would show her that he values her as a person made in his image. Jake had begun to look at other people with God's perspective.

But it was only the first step for him. His mind was becoming a wonderfully clean place—now it was time for him to move on with phase two of his mind renewal diet. It was time for him to renew his mind with right thinking.

Deepak Sharma went on record with the Guinness Book for having sent the most text messages in a single month: 182,689. That's 6,100 messages a day, 253 an hour, 4.2 a minute, or a new one every fourteen seconds or so. So basically this guy gave up a month of his life sending text messages. His other reward? A 1,411 page bill.

LOCK IT DOWN

Now complete these five exercises to apply what you learned in this chapter.

1. Which do you think presents a greater challenge to your mental and spiritual health: the volume of information you consume each day or the content of the information you process? As you make plans for your mental detox, pray that God's Spirit will cleanse your mind of all impurity and help you experience victories in your battle for your mind.

2. Journal your answers to the following questions: How do you feel about the idea of going on a media fast? What challenges do you expect to face, if any? What benefits do you hope to experience? How do you feel about taking every thought captive? What makes this difficult? How will you remind yourself to do this?

3. List all of the media you typically consume in a day, along with the specific purpose you have for consuming it. For example, you might write that you watch the news to stay informed, or that you listen to music to relax and lighten your mood. Or you might say you watch reruns to fill time. Identify the elements of your media consumption that are

absolutely essential and those that are completely optional. Also identify the elements that are somewhere in between.

4. Consider what topics your mind gravitates toward when you have free time. Which topics do you need to clamp down on and eject from your mind? Which topics do you need to capture and meditate on? Develop a system for organizing your free thought life so that you can spend that time focusing on productive or uplifting thoughts. For example, you could make a list on an index card of topics you'd benefit from thinking about. Keep the card in your pocket and refer to it to guide your thinking when you have a few free moments.

5. Write out a specific action plan for your media diet. When will it start and how long will it last? What will you abstain completely from? What types of media will you still need to consume, even during your diet. What limits will you place on the media you do ingest? What specific activities will you engage in to fill the time that's created? Spending time with your family or friends? Developing a new hobby? Completing a project?

Phase 2

REALIGNMENT

WEEK TWO

Practice 3

Consider a New View of You

FOCUS

realign your

beliefs about

yourself to match

God's truth

Have you ever watched the game show *Deal or No Deal*? (Not during your detox time, of course!) Contestants choose one of twenty-six briefcases that they believe holds one million dollars. The game, which requires no skill whatsoever, consists of their choosing and opening cases with various amounts of money and deciding whether or not they truly believe their original unopened case holds the million dollars. A "banker" offers to buy their case for random amounts, further testing their faith in their choice.

It's fascinating to watch these participants, who are supported by friends and family members in the studio audience. Many of them assert, "I believe my case has the million dollars" through the entire game. Of course, their belief has absolutely no bearing whatsoever on the amount of money contained in the case. An ironclad belief cannot change the truth.

> Nurture your mind
> with great thoughts.
>
> —Benjamin Disraeli

Likewise our beliefs about ourselves, solid though they may be, do not affect the truth about who we are. As we move into the second week of the mind renewal diet, we'll focus first on understanding and accepting who we are in God's eyes.

For example, do you say to yourself, "I'm so stupid!" when you make a mistake? If your presentation in the meeting doesn't go well, do you relive your blunders for days afterward? Do you ever think you've got people fooled—that if they knew the real you they'd turn away in disgust? Do you think your spouse deserves someone better than you? Have you ever thought you were a bad parent?

Each of these thoughts reflects a belief system, a pattern of thinking that simply doesn't align with God's truth. It hits us most often when we listen to our feelings instead of what we know to be right. What types of feelings? They could be feelings of helplessness where we feel like we're at the mercy of others, where we have little say in what happens each day, or that living a broken life is our destiny. Sometimes we succumb to feelings of abandonment; we feel isolated, as though we're the only ones who have ever gone through what we're facing and God doesn't hear us. Most detrimental of all are feelings of worthlessness; we feel as though our lives are crumbling around us and we just don't matter—either to God or to the world at large. And feelings of shame; the times we feel as though we've made wrong choices and there is no way to overcome those choices. Feelings that our lives are completely

> Thought, like all potent weapons, is exceedingly dangerous if mishandled. Clear thinking is therefore desirable not only in order to develop the full potentialities of the mind, but also to avoid disaster.
>
> —Giles St. Aubyn

off track by something we've done and there is no way they'll ever get back on track.

Such feelings and the thoughts that go along with them are extremely unhealthy and not easily conquered. However, you can conquer them. Let's learn how.

HOW TO CONQUER DESTRUCTIVE THINKING

We can conquer destructive feelings by identifying them, rejecting them, and replacing them with healthy thoughts. But what does that entail—the idea of healthy or right thinking? Where do healthy thoughts come from? And what should be our criteria for healthy thoughts? Once again, we see that Philippians 4:8 provides a blanket summary: "Whatever is true, whatever is noble, whatever is right, whatever is pure, whatever is lovely, whatever is admirable—if anything is excellent or praiseworthy—think about such things." Perhaps that sounds a little too Peter-Pan-like for you: "Just think happy thoughts and you can fly." Obviously life doesn't work that way, so let's break this idea of changing our view of ourselves down into some key elements.

1. CONFESS YOUR FAILURES AND HARMFUL THOUGHTS

Confession is a glorious thing. Why? Because God already knows what you've done! You're not going to surprise him when you tell him you yelled at your wife and slammed the door on your way out of the house this morning. He already knows you took credit for someone else's idea at work, and he knows that you feel like a worm because of it. He knows what you believe about yourself, that you're unhappy with the direction your life seems to be taking, that you feel out of control. He can hardly wait for you to tell him about it and ask for forgiveness. He longs to release you from the hold those thoughts and actions have on you. And he wants you to know the truth of who you are in him. While you're there, don't forget to ask for help in forgiving those who've hurt you and contributed to your false or negative thought patterns. That's part of breaking free.

> Shame is the only emotion that attacks the self by making one believe that one is inherently defective and unlovable. This crippling emotion destroys self-confidence and prevents one from achieving or enjoying success. When shame pervades one's day-to-day existence, one is torn between one's need to empower and the need to preserve one's relationships.
>
> —Uzma Mazhar

2. DECIDE TO TURN AWAY FROM WRONG THOUGHTS AND BELIEFS

Make a decision to climb out of your rut of negative thinking if for no other reason than you just need to. Absolutely nothing will change if you stay where you are. And you're reading this book because you're looking for positive change. It's sort of like getting on the treadmill. Looking at it won't burn calories. You have to decide to get on it and then do it!

Of course, turning away from something means you're turning toward something else. In this case, it means embracing true thoughts about yourself, considering who you are from God's point of view. Appendix A in this book contains a number of Scriptures for you to read and meditate on so that you can learn more about what God thinks of you. We'll look at some of those a bit later in this chapter.

> As a single footstep will not make a path on the earth, so a single thought will not make a pathway in the mind. To make a deep physical path, we walk again and again. To make a deep mental path, we must think over and over the kind of thoughts we wish to dominate our lives.
>
> —Henry David Thoreau

This decision can also mean turning toward others, considering them and their needs—looking outward rather than inward. When you make a mistake and say, "I'm so stupid," you make others uncomfortable. You put them in the position of having to reassure you, and you also may contribute to their negative thoughts: *If he's so upset about something so small, how will he react if I make a mistake?* Even if you don't say "I'm stupid" out loud, by saying it to yourself, you place unrealistic expectations on yourself and others for the future.

What about when you entertain the thought that your spouse could have done better? Well, let's be real. You're right! However, your spouse chose you. Clearly, your wife saw lovable qualities in you. No doubt your husband saw how you would balance his strengths and weaknesses. By entertaining thoughts of being unworthy of your spouse's love, you cast doubts on that person's abilities to discern, to evaluate, and to love. Put yourself in the other person's place. Would you want your husband to be always looking for assurance that he's worthy to have been chosen? Would you want your wife to thank you constantly for deeming her an acceptable mate? Of course not! Yet, that's what you're doing if you nurture thoughts of not being a worthwhile spouse.

3. FILL YOUR HEART AND MIND WITH RIGHT THOUGHTS

Remember the fundamentals from Philippians 4:8 and apply them. Think about what's lovely in your marriage. Think about what you've done right on the job. What's admirable about your parenting? Refuse negative, counterproductive thinking, and instead align your thinking with God's Word.

WHO I AM IN CHRIST

(Neil Anderson)

If you are a Christian, then the statements below are true of you.[1]

I am accepted.

John 1:12	I am God's child.
John 15:15	As a disciple, I am a friend of Jesus Christ.
Romans 5:1	I have been justified.
1 Corinthians 6:17	I am united with the Lord, and I am one with him in spirit.
1 Corinthians 6:19–20	I have been bought with a price and I belong to God.
1 Corinthians 12:27	I am a member of Christ's body.
Ephesians 1:3–8	I have been chosen by God and adopted as his child.
Colossians 1:13–14	I have been redeemed and forgiven of all my sins.
Colossians 2:9–10	I am complete in Christ.
Hebrews 4:14–16	I have direct access to the throne of grace through Jesus Christ.

I am secure.

Romans 8:1–2	I am free from condemnation.
Romans 8:28	I am assured that God works for my good in all circumstances.
Romans 8:31–39	I am free from any condemnation brought against me and I cannot be separated from the love of God.

2 Corinthians 1:21–22	I have been established, anointed, and sealed by God.
Colossians 3:1–4	I am hidden with Christ in God.
Philippians 1:6	I am confident that God will complete the good work he started in me.
Philippians 3:20	I am a citizen of heaven.
2 Timothy 1:7	I have not been given a spirit of fear, but a spirit of power, love, and a sound mind.
1 John 5:18	I am born of God and the Evil One cannot touch me.

I am significant.

John 15:5	I am a branch of Jesus Christ, the true vine, and a channel of his life.
John 15:16	I have been chosen and appointed to bear fruit.
1 Corinthians 3:16	I am God's temple.
2 Corinthians 5:17–21	I am a minister of reconciliation for God.
Ephesians 2:6	I am seated with Jesus Christ in the heavenly realm.
Ephesians 2:10	I am God's workmanship.
Ephesians 3:12	I may approach God with freedom and confidence.
Philippians 4:13	I can do all things through Christ, who strengthens me.

WHAT GOD SAYS ABOUT YOU

That covers the basics. But it's important to learn how to think about ourselves in a healthy manner. We must have right thoughts about who we are and our place in this world. And we find those foundational thoughts scattered throughout the Bible.

GOD HAS PLANS FOR YOU

Let's start by examining Jeremiah 29:11, where God is speaking to the Israelites and, by extension, all of the people he has chosen for himself, which includes us: "'For I know the plans I have for you,' declares the LORD, 'plans to prosper you and not to harm you, plans to give you hope and a future.'" God has not left us spinning on this earth in some sort of cosmic experiment like laboratory animals in a maze. He is not busy tending to other planets, only checking in on us once in a while. He is not like the leader of your country, busy running the universe, in charge of you but not really cognizant of your presence.

> Every man, at the bottom of his heart, wants to do right. But only he can do right who knows right; only he knows right who thinks right; only he thinks right who believes right.
>
> —Tiorio

Instead, God is intimately interested in each of us. He's interested in me and my life. He's interested in you. He's interested in your life, to the point where he has a plan for it. And it isn't a plan for misery and heartache, either! It's a plan for good things, for provision, for hope and a future.

GOD'S LOVE IS A FREE GIFT

We can turn back several pages in our Bibles to the book of Deuteronomy and get a further glimpse of God's desires for his people. In Deuteronomy 28:8–14, we see more of the way God feels about the people who submit themselves fully to him:

> The LORD will send a blessing on your barns and on everything you put your hand to. The LORD your God will bless you in the land he is giving you.
>
> The LORD will establish you as his holy people, as he promised you on oath, if you keep the commands of the LORD your God and walk in his ways. Then all the peoples on the earth will see that you are called by the name of the LORD, and they will fear you. The LORD will grant you abundant prosperity—in the fruit of your womb, the young of your livestock and the crops of your ground—in the land he swore to your forefathers to give you.
>
> The LORD will open the heavens, the storehouse of his bounty, to send rain on your land in season and to bless all the work of your hands. You will lend to many nations but will borrow from none. The LORD will make you the head, not the tail. If you pay attention to the commands of the

LORD your God that I give you this day and carefully follow them, you will always be at the top, never at the bottom. Do not turn aside from any of the commands I give you today, to the right or to the left, following other gods and serving them.

Now, it's important to note that this comes from the Mosaic law of the Old Testament. For centuries, people did their best to white-knuckle their way to God's love. They worked really, really hard to keep all his commands so they would walk in his provision.

But that isn't the way it works as the apostle Paul clearly spelled out in Galatians 3. Writing to the Galatians, he said in verses 3–5: "Are you so foolish? After beginning with the Spirit, are you now trying to attain your goal by human effort? Have you suffered so much for nothing—if it really was for nothing? Does God give you his Spirit and work miracles among you because you observe the law, or because you believe what you heard?"

Paul then goes on to say in verses 10–14 of the same chapter:

All who rely on observing the law are under a curse, for it is written: "Cursed is everyone who does not continue to do everything written in the Book of the Law" [Deut. 27:26]. Clearly no one is justified before God by the law, because "The righteous will live by faith" [Hab. 2:4].

The law is not based on faith; on the contrary, "The man who does these things will live by them" [Lev. 18:5]. Christ redeemed us from the curse of the law by becoming a curse for us, for it is written: "Cursed is everyone who is hung on a tree" [Deut. 21:23]. He redeemed us in order that the blessing given to Abraham might come to the Gentiles through Christ Jesus, so that by faith we might receive the promise of the Spirit.

It is clear from these passages in Galatians that we don't earn God's love by strict observance of the rules. (And just to clarify, the Israelites didn't earn God's love either; their obedience brought blessing, and their disobedience brought consequences. God's love for his people never wavered.) And how liberating that truth is! That truth is essential to right thinking, to healthy thoughts. It isn't up to us to scratch and claw our way into God's good grace or into a better life here on earth. It is simply up to us to live in obedience as his Spirit enables and empowers us, and to accept God's mercy and grace, which he gives freely.

YOU ARE PART OF A NOBLE COMMUNITY

Look at the types of people that give themselves over to God completely, that fully believe the way he feels about them. We see a little about those people in Hebrews 11, commonly called the Hall of Faith, where the writer of Hebrews runs down a list of people who lived by faith: Abel, Enoch, Noah, Abraham, Isaac, Jacob, Joseph, Moses, Rahab, Gideon, Samson, David, Samuel—the list goes on. It lists person after person who lived a life dedicated to God, fully believing that he loved them and cared about them.

And your name can be on that list too! Remember that God called you. Remember what he did for you—he moved you from the kingdom of darkness into the Kingdom of light when you gave your heart over to him. And as you trust in him and work for his Kingdom, he notes that work in heaven and promises to reward you for it, if not here on earth, then in heaven.

God has promised you a redeemed life, a life called by his grace. He's made spiritual provisions for you, made them all available to you, as we'll see in the next section.

YOU ARE BLESSED IN CHRIST

In the first three chapters of Ephesians, you'll find an extensive list of the blessings God gives his children. Not because we're good. Just because we're his. For example, as a child of God, you are blessed with every spiritual blessing (1:3), chosen (1:4), adopted (1:5), accepted (1:6), and redeemed (1:7). While I don't want to take space to list them all here (since they're easy to find in your Bible), the list of blessings goes on and on, extending throughout the first half of the book of Ephesians.

GOD SENT HIS ONLY CHILD TO RESCUE YOU

God values you that highly. If you need more evidence, look no further than the very famous verses John 3:16–17: "For God so loved the world that he gave his one and only Son, that whoever believes in him shall not perish but have eternal life. For God did not send his Son into the world to condemn the world, but to save the world through him."

God is crazy about the world in general and you in particular. I don't know what sort of relationship you have with your parents, either now or in the past, but one thing that's important to catch about God is that he loves you as a father should love you. Do you have children? If so, you know what I'm talking about. You hold that newborn child, who brings absolutely nothing of benefit to the relationship other than the burdens of feeding and diaper changing, and your heart swells with love. Why? Because that child is yours. For no reason other than that.

And that's the way God feels about you. He loves you, not because of anything you do; He loves you simply because you are his child. What a great way to establish healthy thoughts!

AND THAT IS THE TRUTH!

Once you have the thoughts about yourself straightened out— or at least have started down the road to those healthy self-thoughts (it's probably going to be a lifelong path to walk, reminding your-self how God feels about you), it's important to buoy those thoughts with other healthy thoughts, thinking that complements the truth we've just discussed.

You still need to be taking your thoughts captive, because inevitably your mental input will generate thinking that runs con-trary to the way God feels about you. You will encounter resist-ance to this idea of being God's child—it's only natural. And it's still crucial to capture those thoughts and counter them with what you know about God's love. This is something you'll need to practice for the rest of your life.

In Romans, the Bible calls this practice renewal as we read in chapter 12, verse 2: "Do not conform any longer to the pattern of this world, but be transformed by the renewing of your mind. Then you will be able to test and approve what God's will is—his good, pleasing and perfect will." This is the crux of the mind renewal diet. Renewing your mind helps you determine the ways God wants you to think and act.

When you engage in healthy thoughts by looking into what the Bible says about you and the rest of the world, you're renew-ing your mind and lining it up with God's will. So dig into the Bible, cultivate a substantial prayer life, and you'll find your mind being renewed. You'll find yourself living a life of right, healthy thinking.

DEAR CHILD OF MINE

I love you (John 15:4).

I have called you by name (Isa. 43:1).

You are mine. Before I formed you, I knew you. And before you were born,
I consecrated you (Jer. 1:5).

You did not choose me, I have chosen you (John 15:16).

Because you are precious to me and honored, I love you (Isa. 43:4).

I have loved you with an everlasting love, so I continue to show my constant love (Jer. 31:3).

How could I abandon you? My love for you is too strong (Hos. 11:8).

Can a woman forget her own baby and not love the child she bore? Yet even
should she forget, I can never forget you. See, I have carved you on the
palm of my hand (Isa. 49:15–16).

For I, the Lord your God, am holding you by the right hand (Isa. 41:13).

Do not be afraid; I have redeemed you (Isa. 43:1).

I am with you (Isa. 43:5).

And be sure of this, I am with you *always* until the end of the world (Matt. 28:20).

Do not let your heart be troubled; trust in me (John 14:1).

I will help you (Isa. 41:4).

When you pass through deep waters, I will be with you. Your troubles will
not overwhelm you. The hard trial that comes will not hurt you (Isa. 43:2).

Do not worry (Luke 12:9).

Even the hairs of your head have been numbered, so there is no need to be
afraid of anything (Matt. 10:30).

The mountains may depart and the hills be shaken, but my steadfast love for
you will never end (Isa. 54:10).

Come, I will lead you into solitude, and there I will speak tenderly to
your heart. I will be true and faithful. I will show you constant love
and make you mine forever. I will keep my promise, and you will know
me as never before (Hos. 1:14, 19–20).

I am who I am (Ex. 3:14).

I am the Lord your God (Hos. 13–14).

The faithful God (Hos. 11:12).

I am yours and you are mine (Jer. 7:23).

JAKE'S PROGRESS

How is all this working for Jake? Let's find out. He's just completed his detoxification program, and now he's ready to start building on that foundation. Already he's found that he's being kinder at home, he's enjoying his children more, and his relationship with his wife is stronger than ever. He's spent more time in conversation with everyone in his house over the past two weeks, and it's already begun to reap benefits.

Also, his time away from the demands of media has allowed his devotional life to deepen. He's been digging into the Bible and has uncovered some truths he had forgotten about. He's been consuming the Gospels, specifically studying the words of Jesus. He read that part in Matthew 6 about fasting, and then went on to read the rest of the chapter, landing on verses 25–27:

> Therefore I tell you, do not worry about your life, what you will eat or drink; or about your body, what you will wear. Is not life more important than food, and the body more important than clothes? Look at the birds of the air; they do not sow or reap or store away in barns, and yet your heavenly Father feeds them. Are you not much more valuable than they? Who of you by worrying can add a single hour to his life?

This really resonated with Jake since he'd had those worries about providing for his family. He has begun to zero in on this passage, meditating on it and all it means to him as the head of his household. It has helped him rely more on God for his own strength, and to relax in the comfort that his Heavenly Father cares not only for him but also for his family. Jake is beginning to feel less like someone who has to earn his Father's love and more like someone who is a child of God.

It's showing up in his job performance as well. Now that he's working with a clear mind, with a clear understanding of how God feels about him, he's more confident in his work. No longer driven by an achievement mentality, Jake has relaxed a little and become more enjoyable to be around. He's truly enjoying his time at the office. He's also finding it easier to leave the office on time, and to leave his work mentality at work.

Jake's also been able to continue his practice of taking thoughts into captivity, aware that God has given him a job to do in that respect and that he is completely capable of doing it. No, he doesn't earn his Father's love, but he does need to keep his room clean, so to speak. Having that tidy mind, keeping out all the unhealthy thoughts, is allowing him to walk in victory over sin and has elevated the quality of all areas of his life. Now it's time for him to add something else to the mix: creating a healthy media plan that he can really live with.

LOCK IT DOWN

Now complete these five exercises to apply what you learned in this chapter.

1. During your next time with God, ask him to show you what you believe about yourself. Write down everything that comes to mind as quickly as you can. Be as honest with yourself as you can, and don't worry if it seems negative or silly. Just write. When you can't think of anything else to write, go back and read what you've written. Based on the content of this chapter, how much of your list is consistent with what God thinks about you? If any of your beliefs don't match God's, ask him for guidance on how to replace these false beliefs with the truth. Perhaps you may need to seek the help of your pastor, mentor, or a Christian therapist to help you work through, release, and change your view of yourself.

2. Journal your answers to the following questions: Of the truths you've learned from the Bible about yourself, which do you think is the most important for you to embrace and apply to your life right now? Why? How do you think it would change your life if you were able to genuinely believe and put this truth into practice? What obstacles do

you face in putting this truth to work in your life? How might you overcome these obstacles?

3. Which biblical truth about yourself is easiest for you to believe and provides the most encouragement for you? Find creative ways to remind yourself of this truth in your daily life. Maybe you could purchase or make a sign highlighting the truth to display in your work area or somewhere at home. Or perhaps you could change your computer background or screen saver so that it displays your encouraging message. Since this truth is so meaningful and helpful for you, be sure to make the most of it!

4. Look up the verses in the sidebars of this chapter titled "Who I am in Christ" and "Dear Child of Mine." Choose one of these verses to print on an index card and take it with you wherever you go during the next week. Read it several times a day, meditate on it, and make it a goal to memorize the verse. Doing so will help solidify God's truth in your mind.

5. Read the first three chapters of Ephesians and make a list of all the blessings you find that belong to God's children. Keep your list in a special place and refer to it when you need the encouragement to remember who you are in God's eyes.

Practice 4

Make Mass Media Your Friend

FOCUS

take charge of

the external

influences on

your mind

enjoy Mexican restaurants. Most of them bring a big basket of chips and a bowl of fresh salsa to the table to whet your appetite for the meal to come. But many are the times I've sat down, ordered my food, and then, by the time the food came, realized I'd eaten so many chips that I was no longer hungry for the food I'd ordered!

Taking our restaurant illustration in a slightly different direction, most of us don't sit down at our table and refuse the host's offer of a menu. When our server asks, "What can I get you?" We never say, "Just bring me any old thing. Surprise me." No, we want to spend our money on something we're pretty sure we're going to enjoy.

Unfortunately, most of us tend to be less disciplined and discriminating in our media consumption. We'll sit down in front of the TV or computer or open a magazine or book, and by our actions say, "Surprise me." Instead of snacking briefly and moving on to a well-balanced meal of social, intellectual, and spiritual nourishment, we overindulge on the appetizer until we finally look away from the computer or TV screen and see that it's past bedtime and we haven't made time for the actual meal.

At this point in your journey with renewing your mind, I hope that you are already beginning to see some changes in the way that you think. The reason that a media fast, or detoxification plan, is such an important part of the early stages of the mind renewal diet is because mass media has such a significant (and often covert) impact on the way we think. As we begin to limit and manage the massive amounts of information that we take in through various media and focus our intake on healthier content, it is bound to make a difference in the way our minds function. I trust you've also been working hard to regulate the internal functioning of your mind, so that you are capturing those thoughts that bubble up from within your own heart, ejecting the unhealthy ones and embracing the healthy. Also, you're now filling your mind with healthy thoughts and concepts like those we discussed in the previous chapter.

Many Web sites offer movie reviews based on biblical principles and from a Christian perspective. Below is a sample:

http://www.pluggedinonline.com
http://www.christiananswers.net/spotlight
http://www.christianitytoday.com/movies
http://www.crosswalk.com/movies
http://www.movieguide.org

Now there's no excuse for being surprised by a movie's content!

Now it's time to add another layer to your mind renewal diet. We need to work together to establish a healthy meal plan, if you will, for your media intake. We need to create a healthy mass

One shining example of the power of order in music is King George I of England. King George had problems with memory loss and stress management. He learned from the Bible that King Saul had experienced the same type of problems that he was experiencing, and that Saul overcame his problems by using special music. With this story in mind King George asked George Frederick Handel to write some special music for him that would help him in the same way that music helped Saul. Handel wrote his Water Music for this purpose.

media regimen that you can actually abide by and that will leave you with the mental energy and metabolism you need to live the best life you can.

Again, we start with Philippians 4:8: "Whatever is true, whatever is noble, whatever is right, whatever is pure, whatever is lovely, whatever is admirable—if anything is excellent or praiseworthy—think about such things."

I have to make a confession. Even though I've referred to it numerous times, sometimes I get a little peeved with this verse. I think that it must have been so much easier for the early Christians to put it into practice. After all, they didn't have TV, movie theaters, DVD players, satellite dishes, magazines, iPods, or the Internet. They had never even heard of an electrical outlet or an on/off switch! However, in doing the research for this book, I've changed my thinking about it being more difficult for us than it was for our first century brothers and sisters in Christ. Since you may have had similar feelings (even if you don't want to admit them), I'll share some of what I learned that changed my mind.

ANCIENT MASS MEDIA OPTIONS

The ancient world offered plenty of entertainment options, although most required leaving home and even traveling to the next town. It might surprise you to learn that Jesus lived very near a major entertainment venue. In little more than an hour, if he had so chosen, Jesus could have walked from his home in Nazareth to the nearby city of Sepphoris to attend a show in a four thousand-seat Roman-style amphitheater built by Herod Antipas.[1] Such venues were scattered throughout the world in the days of the early church, and many people took advantage of the entertainment they offered. People attending the theater might see a comedy (farce), a tragedy, or even a mime. However, in going to such a performance, a person risked exposure to lewd and bawdy sex and possibly real-life violence.[2]

If the theater wasn't your idea of fun, you could always go to the Coliseum in Rome, or one of the many other smaller stadia dotting the Roman Empire, to watch animal fights (some estimate that five thousand animals were killed on opening day at the Coliseum[3]) or a little hand-to-hand combat between gladiators, in which the winner killed the loser. In his book *Confessions*, Augustine of Hippo describes the powerful fascination and temptation such entertainment held for the average person, including himself, and how he eventually experienced victory over the temptation.

Or, to avoid the crowds yet still have some fun, a first-century man could always find a respectable game of dice on the street. Of course, participating meant gambling with your family's possessions.

Added to all of that, the writings of early Christians and others make it crystal clear that they too wrestled with the interior assaults of their own minds. Thoughts presented themselves without summons, and they were left to wrestle with and figure out what to do with them.

So even though our entertainment options are significantly different today, it would be a mistake to think that the early Christians somehow had it easier than we do or that it was much simpler for them to engage only in activities that helped them think thoughts that were in keeping with Philippians 4:8.

If you're looking for a list of specific suggestions about what to watch, read, or listen to, take a look at Appendix B at the end of this book. There you'll find listed a variety of books, movies, and music that I recommend for just about any taste. Those are specifics. In the rest of this chapter we're going to apply the basic principles of Philippians 4:8 to a variety of different media.

TV AND MOVIES

Let's start with television and movies. What type of viewing do you like to do? Reality shows in prime time? Animal shows on The Discovery Channel? Documentaries on PBS? Twenty-four-hour news channels? Twenty-four-hour movie channels? Twenty-four-hour sports or gardening channels? With all the channels available via cable and home satellite dishes—as well as a record number of movie screens seemingly at every corner—we have more options for entertainment than ever before.

Evaluating what we watch begins with examining our motives: Why do we want to watch what we want to watch? Here are some possible healthy motivations for watching a particular TV program:

- to be uplifted and inspired to live a better life;

- to learn something that will help me solve a problem in my life;

- to understand more about people and how relationships work;

- to stretch my mind or see life from a different perspective;

- to keep informed about what's going on in the world around me.

And here are some possible unhealthy motivations for watching TV:

- to kill time so I don't have to engage with the world around me;

- to drown out the silence;

- to get a buzz or to experience a vicarious thrill;

- to avoid doing something I really need to do;

- to experience intimacy with people on TV rather than developing real relationships.

Examine your heart to determine the motivations behind what you watch and you'll have a much firmer foundation for developing a healthy mass media meal plan. You can build time for TV into your media meal plan in moderation when you have healthy reasons for watching, but ruthlessly eliminate from your media diet any TV watching that stems from unhealthy motivations.

Sometimes our motivations can't easily be classified as healthy or unhealthy, and that's okay. For example, you might say, "I just want to be entertained for a while" or "I just don't have the energy for anything else right now." There's nothing necessarily wrong with watching TV for these reasons. Just be sure that you limit the amount of time you watch TV for such reasons and don't use such statements as an excuse for watching programs that feed unhealthy thoughts to your mind.

Watching TV can be a healthy activity, but it is not naturally so. Without a plan for healthy viewing, it can very easily become an activity that undermines your efforts to have a healthy and pure thought life.

MUSIC

Now let's turn our attention to music. Music is a powerful medium because it connects with our spirits in a way that no other form of media does. Music speaks directly to our souls in a language that is more emotional than intellectual. That's one reason movies always have a soundtrack. The musical score gives us nonverbal cues about how the director wants us to feel about the action we're seeing on the screen. And, most often, we follow the director's musical instructions.

Without music, we can view an ordinary, ambiguous scene of a person walking up stairs and think nothing of it. Add a soundtrack, though, and the director can tell us through music how we should be feeling. Put ominous, low strings, punctuated with high strings or ethereal piano, and suddenly we're worried for the person. Is she walking into a trap? Put energetic, cheerful strings running joyous arpeggios, a full orchestra with soaring woodwinds, and suddenly we're happy for the person. We're certain he'll find his long-lost love at the top of the stairs. The wildly different musical cues can lend completely different interpretations to the exact same visual.

Maybe you're feeling especially courageous and want to expand your listening to include classical music. Check out *Music of the Great Composers* by Patrick Cavanaugh for a guided tour through the world of classical music from a Christian perspective. The book includes an appendix titled "A Lifetime of Listening: Your First Thousand Pieces" to get you started in the various sub-genres of classical music (symphonies, choral works, solo instrumental works, and so forth).

Music is such a powerful influence on our thoughts and emotions that it's important for us to carefully examine why we like to listen to the music we listen to. Is it simply because you have an appreciation for that style of music, or is there something deeper? How do you feel when you listen to a particular style of music? Do you feel peaceful and energized, or are you left angry and depressed? Does it turn your thoughts toward God and his kingdom or away?

There is no right style of music; I prefer certain styles and artists, obviously, but I'm not going to tell you that you have to listen exclusively to what I enjoy. But your choice in music is important all the same because of how it impacts your thoughts. When you listen to music, you are giving the composer and performer access to your mind in a way that has unique staying power. If you want to be successful in your mental diet, pay attention to the types of music that you take in each day. Choose to listen to music that will aid you in your efforts to keep a clean mind and pure heart rather than making it more of a challenge.

WORDS IN PRINT

Let's move on to the written word, which we see primarily in the form of books, magazines, newspapers, and the like. Depending on your age, you may have been told, when you were growing up, that reading in itself is great. "Read a book," those posters in your school library implored. The underlying message was "just read something, please. We're losing kids to TV, and we don't like it."

But what you read is just as important as that you read. Putting information in a book doesn't automatically make it good, useful, and beneficial. Not everything you read in books is true, and not everything you read is worth reading. There are self-help books packed with stale platitudes that were only put onto the page to take up room and make the book thicker so the publisher can charge you more for it. There are books, even in Christian book stores, that run counter to God's Word and were only written because someone had to fulfill a contract with a publisher. That's why it's so important to be discerning in what you choose to read.

The same is true for reading magazines. There are magazines that will educate, inform, and inspire you in a variety of ways. For many years, the likes of *Time*, *Newsweek*, and *U.S. News and World Report* dominated the news magazine market. With more and more people turning to the Internet for their day-to-day information, such magazines are struggling to maintain their readership. Many magazines have been forced to specialize in order to survive. Now there are magazines for just about every hobby or profession, no matter how small the niche might be. There's also a lot of junk, and the junk never seems to stop multiplying.

Newspapers are about as benign as it gets in the media world. Even there, though, the reader must beware the reporter's unique slant and biases. Objective reporting is a loose term and it can be difficult or even impossible for a reporter to write a story without letting personal bias show through. Plus, newspapers have always been fond of shocking, attention-grabbing headlines and have a tendency to create news where there is none. Ever hear of a slow news day? They still print the paper, don't they? So, even with newspapers, it's important to be on your guard and watchful for any unhealthy thoughts it might plant in your brain.

With printed media, the question we must ask ourselves, once again, is "Why?" Why are we interested in reading the material we typically read? Are we reading a particular book because it's a classic, or because we secretly hope it will have some shocking or heart-rate-quickening content that will then be okay because we read it in a book? Are we reading that magazine because we like the content of the articles or because we're bored in the waiting room at the doctor's office? Are we reading the newspaper because we need to know what's going on in the world or just because that's what we've always done? Choose reading material that will support your goal of developing and maintaining a clean and pure thought life.

> All the problems of the world could be settled easily if men were only willing to think. The trouble is that men very often resort to all sorts of devices in order not to think, because thinking is such hard work.
>
> —Thomas J. Watson

INTERNET

Interestingly, the Internet has become one-stop shopping for all types of media. There are entire sites devoted to news. In fact, your favorite newspaper probably has an online component. Most television networks have Web sites with clips from their shows or even entire episodes. There's an entire industry devoted to delivery of music over the Internet, and there are many Web sites that offer streaming radio for you to listen to at work. And then there are the ultra-popular video Web sites that feature clips of just about everything ever shown on a screen.

So why are you on the Internet? Most people go online because they're bored or just because they always go on the Internet. Very few of us actually open our browser for a specific reason, find what we wanted to find, and then close our browser immediately. Even if we log on for a specific reason (to check our e-mail, for example), we hardly ever stop there. We're like the children in the old *Family Circus* comic strip who wander through the back door into the house, stop in the living room to grab a toy, go up to the bedroom to pet the cat, walk into the kitchen to get a drink, and then leave through the front door, only to remember that they'd gone into the house to ask Mom a question.

At the risk of trying the reader's patience, the question is still, you guessed it, "Why?" Why are you visiting the sites you're visiting? Do you need each of them for a purpose other than curiosity? Why are you spending so much time on the Internet in general? Do you literally have nothing else to do? Why are you so eager to check your e-mail? Are you secretly expecting a new message from someone to validate your existence?

The questions can range far and wide, and they don't always have to have suspicious answers. You may have a

> If you read a lot of books, you are considered well read. But if you watch a lot of TV, you're not considered well viewed.
>
> —Lily Tomlin

legitimate reason to check your e-mail every five minutes. (Perhaps you're trying to arrange last-minute dinner plans and are checking to see if anyone has sent you an RSVP.)

Your reasons for engaging with any type of media don't all have to be lofty and grand, either. Maybe you've just finished mowing the back forty on a hot Saturday afternoon. Your spouse was gracious enough to provide you with a glass of ice-cold lemonade, and you've already flopped onto the couch to enjoy it. Is it okay to turn on the TV to check on the game? Sure! You don't have to spend an hour searching your soul for motivation or wonder what would Jesus do. And once you've developed a healthy meal plan—knowing what to consume and in what quantities, as well as what to avoid—you won't need to spend nearly as much time thinking through every decision you make about media. As effortlessly as you fall asleep when you're exhausted, you'll change the channel when a show comes on that will pose too great a temptation for your mind. The goal is to develop healthy habits, so that such decisions are a breeze.

Even then, it's good to remember that relationships should always come first. After you flop on the couch to watch the game, maybe you notice that your wife is still standing next to you. Take a quick emotional pulse of the situation. What does she need right now? Does she need to ask you a question? Do you need to ask what's on her mind? (Is she simply waiting for you to say thank you?!) Even if she doesn't come right out and tell you what she needs, be sure to pay attention to the nonverbal cues she's sending. There's absolutely nothing wrong with flipping on the game, but remember that people need to come first.

PRACTICAL HELP FOR TAKING CHARGE OF YOUR MEDIA INTAKE

Maybe you're not the most introspective person in the world, and all this talk about considering your motives is making you a little nervous. While motivation is primary, it doesn't stand alone. Following are some concrete ways for you to be the boss of your media intake.

PLAN

There's no substitute for having a meal plan for your media consumption. Take an inventory of your current involvement with various forms of media. Decide what changes you'd like to see in your consumption patterns. Determine what you will do and what you won't do from here on out. Write out your plan, and then stick to it.

SET A TIME LIMIT

Have you ever kept track of how much TV you watch in a week? How about how much time you spend looking at and answering e-mail? Consider setting time limits for yourself. For example, you're only going to watch TV at certain times or on certain days; you're only going to read the paper on Sundays; you'll spend no more than an hour a day on e-mail (or whatever is truly appropriate for your job). Or, check your e-mail at the top of the hour rather than every time you hear a sound announcing you have new mail. Listen to music only when you're doing housework or making dinner. Then ask God to help you stick to your limits.

CREATE FILTERS

If you have cable or satellite TV, you can create locks for content and specific channels. If you tend to spend your weekend channel surfing from movie to movie, create a channel list that blocks or limits those channels.

Set up filters and mailboxes for e-mails from specific people or messages that contain certain key words. For example, if you receive daily sales reports, set up a mailbox for those documents so you won't be tempted to look at them the moment they pop into your inbox.

PURGE

If you have inappropriate music on your iPod, delete it! If you're tempted to spend a lot of time playing Solitaire on your computer, delete it! If your DVD collection or fiction library contains movies or books that don't meet the Philippians 4:8 standards, dump them. This is a no-brainer, but it's essential for your mind's health.

Are you considering whether your media is true, noble, right, pure, lovely, admirable, excellent, or praiseworthy, or are you just taking whatever the world dishes out to you? Are you taking control of your media intake or is your media intake taking control of you?

JAKE'S PROGRESS

Jake really enjoyed and benefited from his media fast, but since the detoxification process ended, he's allowing his intake of mass media to creep back toward its previous levels, growing slightly every day. He still isn't watching as much television as he had in the past, and he's mostly spending his drive time in prayer, though he occasionally turns on the radio. But Jake's biggest problem is with the Internet.

Jake has recently found himself using the Internet for no real reason. He'll hit up his favorite sports Web sites and read everything they have available, even about sports he has never really followed. He finds himself visiting a news Web site and consuming entertainment news that means nothing to him. And his Achilles' heel has become fantasy football.

In years past, the rapidly growing pastime has been a fun diversion for Jake, but he now finds himself spending more and more time reading up on the fantasy football world. He's starting to pay more attention to the television on Sunday afternoons, hoping to catch a glimpse of the stat lines of different players so he can gauge how his team is performing that day.

> Reading is a means of thinking with another person's mind; it forces you to stretch your own.
> —Charles Scribner, Jr.

During the week, he visits several fantasy football Web sites to read up on player injuries and to get advice from fantasy football experts about which players should have statistically good games and which players should have statistically bad games. He spends time on the Web site for his own league, looking at the reservoir of available players in the hopes of bolstering his own lineup.

Fantasy sports have suddenly become less of a pastime and more of an obsession for Jake, because his team has been performing well and he finds himself in a position of potentially winning the entire league. There's no money at stake—he's playing just for the fun of it—but his desire to win, his overwhelming competitive nature, is making itself manifest in his life and in his mind.

Now he's spending time away from the computer thinking about his lineup. In years past, he would wait until the end of the day Sunday to check his scores to see how his team had performed; now he's dialing up scores on his cell phone every few minutes, no matter where he and his family are.

But Jake is checking his heart motivation, and he's finding that he has allowed himself to become too attached to this pastime. It has stopped being about having fun, and it has become about winning. But he doesn't want to let his team languish; that wouldn't be fair to the rest of the friends he plays with.

After praying about it considerably, Jake figures out a way to bring that obsession back into balance by trimming away all the extra time he spends doing research on players and reading commentary. He asks God to examine that part of his heart and change it so that he can have a cleaner, healthier mind. After a few weeks of this, he finds that his heart has changed and that his priorities are once more back in order. He has more time for his family and for himself, which is great, because now he's going to focus on surrounding himself with positive people.

LOCK IT DOWN

Now complete these five exercises to apply what you learned in this chapter.

1. Take a media inventory. (You can find a Media Inventory Worksheet in Appendix C of this book.) For one week, list everything that you watch, listen to, or read, along with the amount of time that you spend with each activity. At the end of the week, mark whether each item contributed healthy thoughts, unhealthy thoughts, or mixed thoughts (a mixture of healthy and unhealthy thoughts). Total up how much time you spent feeding your mind healthy, unhealthy, and mixed thoughts.

2. Create a media meal plan for the upcoming week. (You can find a Media Meal Plan Worksheet in Appendix D of this book.) List what media you plan to consume in the upcoming week, along with how much time you plan to spend on that activity. As you follow the plan you've created, mark where your actual media consumption differed from your plan. What can you learn from these differences?

3. Journal the answers to the following questions: What do you wrestle most with in terms of media consumption. In what areas are you already experiencing victory? What do you

expect will be the most difficult type of media for you to bring under control? What changes do you plan to make to make mass media your friend?

4. Consider how you might combine making media consumption a social event.

- Take your family or friends out to a concert and for ice cream afterward.

- If you have young children, read a book to them at an unexpected time of day (after breakfast). You'll be filling their minds with what's good, and everybody will benefit from the extra snuggle time. (If you don't have young children but know some, their parents would be thrilled to have you borrow them for story time!)

- Plan your next remodeling or landscaping project online with your spouse.

- Watch your spouse's (or child's or teenager's or best friend's) favorite movie together. Make popcorn, pile up the pillows and blankets, and enjoy time together. If you like action flicks and she likes Broadway musicals, or if he's a big WWII documentary fan and you're a connoisseur of all things Oscar, you'll shock the other person by suggesting the idea and make him or her feel loved and appreciated.

5. Review your progress on the mind renewal diet. What is going well? What's not going as well? Make note of how your thinking has changed since you began. What additional progress would you like to make in the future? What kinds of adjustments do you need to make in order to make that happen?

Surround Yourself with Positive People

FOCUS

choose to

spend time with

people who

raise the bar

My old friend Zig Ziglar often says, "I don't want to hang around people who brighten the room when they leave it; I want to hang around people who brighten the room when they enter it!" I feel the same way!

Remember Jack Nicholson's great line in *As Good as It Gets*? In that movie Nicholson plays an obnoxious, self-centered, obsessive-compulsive jerk with the tiniest spark of humanity visible on only rare occasions. Helen Hunt, a waitress who at least tolerates him and his odd and annoying behaviors, asks him to tell her what he likes about her. He fidgets and stutters for a few moments and then blurts out, "You make me want to be a better man." Those are the people you and I need to seek out; individuals who make us want to be better husbands, wives, friends, parents, and Christians.

> There is little difference in people, but that little difference makes a big difference. The little difference is attitude. The big difference is whether it is positive or negative.
>
> —W. Clement Stone

I once heard a well-known and successful celebrity—in music and movies—talk about the difference between those who remain in a mind-set of poverty and deprivation and those who overcome it. She said something along these lines: "When I go back to my old neighborhood, I see some of the same people standing on the same street corners, hanging out with the same friends they've had since they were ten years old. They'll probably be there until they're old men. I chose to surround myself with people who had goals and dreams similar to mine. We would get together and try out our new music on each other, helping each other refine and develop what we'd written. We'd encourage each other to reach for our dreams, and we wouldn't let anybody back down. That's a big part of how I got to be where I am today."

It's so easy in our culture to allow negative and destructive thinking to permeate our speech and relationships. We criticize the boss because that's what everybody else is doing. We complain about our taxes or our spouse or our car because it's just what people do. It's a quick and often comfortable way to make conversation. But now that we've taken the time to clean up our minds, we don't want to refill them with negative and critical words that will pollute them again. In this chapter, we're going to look at ways to live the mind renewal diet out loud through our daily interactions with people.

> The average pencil is seven inches long, with just a half-inch eraser— in case you thought optimism was dead.
>
> —Robert Brault

LOOK FOR LIGHTNING BUGS

If you got to spend even a few days of your summer outside the city, chances are you and your friends tried to catch lightning bugs in the evening after dinner. You'd grab an old peanut butter jar, poke holes in the lid, and race to be the first one to capture one of the glowing beetles.

Medical research has shown that positive people have unusually good health and avoid many of the illnesses that other people tend to go through. Their bodies appear to have a much higher stamina level and a better ability to fight disease and they usually live longer than the people who allow their lives to be lead by negativity.

Just as lightning bugs attracted us when we were children, positive people attract others. Take a moment to consider individuals at work or at church who seem to always have an encouraging word or choose to see the sunny side of a problem or situation. I'm not talking about people who walk around saying, "Praise God! I have an ulcer!" or "Hallelujah! I totaled my car yesterday." That's not realistic or even particularly Christlike. I'm talking about people who look at problems as opportunities or challenges; people who say, "The missions budget is short this month? Let's talk to God about it and then see what we can do" or "The boss seems really stressed today. How can I encourage him or lighten his load?" These are the individuals to look for, to seek out, and to befriend.

To better describe the qualities of positive people, let's take a look at a biblical example of lightning bugs.

> We gain nothing by being with such as ourselves. We encourage one another in mediocrity. I am always longing to be with men more excellent than myself.
>
> —Charles Lamb

BARNABAS GLOWED

The New Testament book of Acts chronicles the beginning of the church, highlighting God's work through individuals as the body of Christ is born and grows. One of those people was Joseph. We know him better by the name the apostles gave him, Barnabas, which means Son of Encouragement (Acts 4:36).

Here are a few of the ways Barnabas encouraged others.

BARNABAS WAS GENEROUS (ACTS 4:36–37)

To be sure, Barnabas was not the only member of the early church who sold his property and gave his income to the church. But the fact that he did so tells us something important about the character of this man of God, as well as all of those who genuinely encourage others. He was not self-centered, but other-centered. He did not attempt to gain for himself, but gave sacrificially for others. In other words, Barnabas was a generous person. This was true of his finances and it was also true in the way he related with others.

BARNABAS GAVE PAUL A CHANCE (ACTS 9:24–27)

While others were reluctant or anxious or downright frightened to welcome Paul into the community of believers, Barnabas courageously stood up for him and spoke on his behalf, urging the disciples to receive him into fellowship. It reminds me of when Jesus reached out his hand to touch a leper. Both Jesus and Barnabas were willing to get their hands dirty in order to lift up another person. Imagine how different Church history might look today if it had not been for Barnabas giving Paul a chance!

BARNABAS SUPPORTED THE WORK OF THE KINGDOM (ACTS 11:19–26)

Barnabas was sent by the church to follow up with a group of Christians at Antioch who had begun sharing the gospel with Greeks and having great success too. Verses 23–24 say that "When he [Barnabas] arrived and saw the evidence of the grace of God, he was glad and encouraged them all to remain true to the Lord with all their hearts. He was a good man, full of the Holy Spirit and faith, and a great number of people were brought to the Lord." Not only that, but Barnabas then went and found Paul and brought him to Antioch. Together they spent a whole year with the new Christians, encouraging them and helping them grow in their faith. With one stroke, Barnabas strengthened the church at Antioch and helped Paul find and engage in a fruitful and productive new ministry.

BARNABAS GAVE JOHN MARK A SECOND CHANCE (ACTS 15:36–41)

We've already seen Barnabas give Paul a shot. Now he gives John Mark a second chance over the objections of Paul. John Mark had joined Paul and Barnabas on their first missionary journey, but abandoned them to return home before their mission was completed. Paul was dead set against taking John Mark with them the next time, but Barnabas was just as determined to give him a second chance. Barnabas placed a higher priority on encouraging John Mark in his ministry than continuing to work with

There is no such thing as a "self-made" man. We are made up of thousands of others. Everyone who has ever done a kind deed for us or spoken one word of encouragement to us, has entered into the makeup of our character and of our thoughts, as well as our success.

—George Matthew Adams

Paul, and thus two new missionary teams were born. Paul took Silas, and Barnabas took John Mark.

Len Sweet, in his book *11*, paints this practical picture of a Barnabas:

> A Barnabas is . . . someone to hold up those tired and weary arms; someone to add a hand when you rarely or barely hear the sound of one hand clapping; someone who gives you permission to fail, permission to write a bad first draft; someone who can remind you that God gives us a portion adequate for us to make it through the day; . . . someone who, when life takes your breath away and you hold it in, will slap your back and "inspire" you with the enlivening Spirit that makes you want to breathe again; someone who will lift you up when you're road-whipped, world-weary, bone-tired, blood-thin, when you feel buttonholed and browbeaten; someone who will encourage you when you're tempted to think that the only difference between yogurt and the church you're a part of is that yogurt has active, living culture.[1]

> Persons are judged to be great because of the positive qualities they possess, not because of the absence of faults.
> —Author Unknown

Barnabas was an encouragement in both his actions and words, in his genuineness, and in his example of Christian living. He was an encouragement because he was real, he lived it out, and when others saw him, they were inspired and encouraged.

Perhaps by now you're ready to go searching for your Barnabas. Or maybe you're a little intimidated at the thought of trying to find a friend or colleague who measures up to the biblical Barnabas. Remember that at the beginning of the chapter we talked about people who raise you up, who make you want to be a better person? Barnabas is an excellent example of just that kind of person. Now, of course, the question is, where have all the Barnabases gone?

> He who walks with the wise grows wise, but a companion of fools suffers harm.
>
> —Proverbs 13:20

FINDING BARNABAS

You might have noticed that the heading above doesn't say "Waiting for Barnabas" or "Wishing for Barnabas." That's because it's not very often you'll respond to a knock on the door and hear the words, "Hi, I'm here to be your Barnabas. I want to build you up and motivate you to live a better life. Let's get started!"

We can only surround ourselves with positive people by going to where the positive people are! That said, the first place to look for positive people is right on your nightstand (or wherever it is you keep your Bible). The person who best demonstrated all the qualities you're looking for was Jesus Christ! That's not to say he was all daisies and rainbows. No, he said, "In this world you will have trouble." But with hardly a breath between sentences, he went right on to say, "But take heart! I have overcome the world" (John 16:33). Start reading the Gospels, looking for ways Jesus wants to build you up, to increase your faith and hope, to make you more like him.

The next step in surrounding yourself with positive people is prayer. To quote Jesus again: "Your Father knows what you need before you ask him" (Matt. 6:8). God already knows you need people in your life that strengthen and encourage you and help you direct your focus toward him. He's already made provision for you. But he still wants you to talk with him about it. Ask him to open your eyes to positive individuals at work, at church, or in other places you frequent. Then ask him to show you how best to interact with

> What a great favor God does to those he places in the company of good people.
>
> —Teresa of Ávila

them. Do you need to invite someone out for coffee and ask how he keeps his mind focused on the positive? Do you need to start a Bible study for you and a couple others who want to develop a deeper relationship with the Lord? Have you thought about asking someone to mentor you in this area?

Once you've asked God to show you the Barnabases he has for you, anticipate a positive outcome! You can be sure you're praying within his will when you ask this. Jesus said, "Whatever you ask for in prayer, believe that you have received it, and it will be yours" (Mark 11:24). (Of course, I'm not suggesting you use this verse to claim a million dollars and a Lamborghini. However, I believe it applies to what we know to be God's will for us—developing the mind of Christ, aligning our desires with his, a greater love for him and his people, and so forth.) Believe that he wants to bring into your life those who will build you up and strengthen your faith, and then believe he has already answered your prayer.

Let's see how practice five is working for Jake.

JAKE'S PROGRESS

Jake feels pretty blessed to have a wife who supports him in his mind renewal diet. He knows he's been up and down, and his progress hasn't been completely steady—he's had his share of setbacks. Of course, she's been participating in the mental diet as well, and she hasn't been perfect either. But it's been interesting to see how God has kept them from being discouraged at the same time. When Laurie's been down, Jake's been able to remind her of the value of what they're doing, and when Jake's struggled, Laurie has encouraged him with words of praise for the benefits his perseverance is bringing to their marriage and family.

Jake knows, though, that he can't look to his wife to be his only source of encouragement. That's a lot to expect from any one person. He knows he needs to cultivate positive friendships outside the home as well.

For starters, Jake has decided to reread the Gospels, this time looking specifically for how Jesus encouraged his disciples and others who heard him speak. In fact, he went out and purchased an inexpensive red-letter Bible just so he can find Jesus' words quickly and then highlight those that especially stand out.

On his drive to work this morning, he asked God to show him a positive person he can get to know a little better. The environment in his office isn't usually the most upbeat, but Jake knows God is bigger than environments and circumstances.

Armed with his new perspective, and feeling like he was on some sort of mission, Jake made it a point to listen to various conversations as he made his way to his desk that morning and then later in the lunchroom. He wasn't eavesdropping for information, just trying to hear how people talked about their weekends and the work facing them in the coming week, listening for coworkers that approach life with a more positive outlook, for potential Barnabases.

On the drive home, Jake fought off discouragement. He had observed and prayed throughout the day, but had not really found someone that stood out as a positive person, one with the qualities Jake was seeking for.

The rest of the week, Jake continued to pray for a person who would come alongside him and be his Barnabas.

The following Sunday night at their couples' small group meeting, Jake worked up the courage to tell the others what he'd been praying for. When he finished, the group remained silent. Finally one of the guys said, "Jake, I've been praying for the same thing for a couple of months now." A couple other men nodded.

By the end of the evening, an offshoot of the small group had formed. Three guys planned to meet for lunch every Tuesday for the purpose of encouraging and praying for one another. Jake knew it wasn't exactly a great cloud of witnesses, but it was a pretty good start, and he thanked God for answering his prayer.

LOCK IT DOWN

Now complete these five exercises to apply what you learned in this chapter.

1. Make a list of all the people that you can think of in your life, past and present, that have been an encouragement to you. Write down their names and, if you can remember, specific examples of how they have encouraged you. Pray and thank God for bringing such people into your life when you need them. Then choose one or two of the people on your list and write a thank you note telling them what a blessing and gift from God they were to you.

2. Journal your answers to the following questions: Who are the most encouraging people that you see on a regular basis? How have they encouraged you personally? How much do you need additional encouragement in your life right now? How many people do you think would identify you as a source of encouragement in their lives? Who do you know that needs a Barnabas in their life right now? How will you help meet that need?

3. Do you need encouragement in your life right now? Try praying that God will give you the opportunity to encourage someone else today. Sometimes the best encouragement you can receive flows from being an encouragement to others.

4. Where are you in your quest to surround yourself with positive people? Reading? Praying? Expecting? What do you need to do to move forward? Write down your plan and take small steps toward accomplishing it each day.

5. Barnabas wasn't the only encourager in the New Testament. Read about Onesiphorus in 2 Timothy 1:16–18. Why was Paul so thankful for Onesiphorus? What did he do that meant so much to Paul? Who are the Onesiphoruses in your life? How can you be an Onesiphorus for others?

REINFORCEMENT

WEEK THREE

Practice 6

Create a Circle of Accountability

FOCUS

long-term

success on the mind

renewal diet requires

accountability

When it comes to dieting and losing weight, one key element causes your odds of success to go sky high: accountability. Whether you go to structured meetings or check in with a friend informally via phone or e-mail, having someone else in your corner strengthens your resolve and elevates your capabilities beyond their normal capacity. In addition to having someone cheer you on in your efforts, an accountability partner can also help trace your progress, making sure you stay on track.

Think of a commercial airplane. From the time the plane leaves its gate in one city to the time it arrives at its destination gate, the flight crew is in continuous contact with a key person on the ground, the air traffic controller. The air traffic controller's job is to make sure the plane stays on course and to assist the crew in safely navigating the plane to its destination. The pilot is flying the plane, but the air traffic controller keeps the pilot accountable for following the approved flight plan.

A diet (or a flight) is a large undertaking. A thought diet even more so. It is essentially exchanging one way of life for another, and it's a load that's best not to shoulder alone. There is just too much temptation to give up or give in. When someone else helps you bear the burden of your thought diet, even though you won't eliminate temptation completely, you'll receive reinforcement and encouragement and a little extra incentive to stay on course, since you know someone will be asking. As you launch into your third week of the mind renewal diet, make it a goal to find an accountability partner, someone who will provide the necessary encouragement and support to help you stick to your new commitments. But first, let's focus on an accountability partner who is already in place and waiting for the opportunity to support you in your endeavor.

"People who come to Weight Watchers meetings lose three times more weight than those who go it alone."

(As reported in the April 2003 issue of the *Journal of the American Medical Association* 289[14]:1792.)

TWO KINDS OF ACCOUNTABILITY

For the Christian, there are two kinds of accountability: accountability to God and accountability to fellow Christians. Accountability to God most often happens on an internal level as you communicate and converse with the Lord of creation through prayer. The psalmist David illustrates the accountability a person can find in relationship to God in this beautiful and exemplary prayer: "Search me, O God, and know my heart; test me and know my anxious thoughts. See if there is any offensive way in me, and

> Authentic accountability with each other could be the very thing that re-ignites our passion for Christ and his kingdom. This is certainly true when we find ourselves seeking accountability because of a moral failing. In becoming known to others *in Christ*, our unity and love for each other could become a significant part of our healing, making it safe and genuinely attractive for non-Christians to explore the reality of Christian fellowship.
>
> —Rob Jackson

lead me in the way everlasting" (Ps. 139:23–24). That's a prayer that any of us can learn to pray, and it's a perfect fit for someone who is journeying through the mind renewal diet, as you are. Let it remind you that you are accountable to God for the health of your mind, and expect God to answer your prayer.

For many centuries, Christians have engaged in a spiritual exercise called the *Prayer of Examen*. It can be traced back as far as Ignatius of Loyola, but it's possible that it goes back even further. The Prayer of Examen is more or less a way to conduct a spiritual self-review in the presence of God. Google the term *Prayer of Examen* and you'll find plenty of resources online to help you learn about praying this prayer. (Use your critical thinking skills, of course, to choose the Web sites that most closely adhere to a Biblical perspective on the Christian faith.)

The basic elements involved in this ancient Christian practice are: acknowledging the presence of God in your life, expressing gratitude to God for his goodness to you, reviewing together with

God the last twenty-four hours of your life, and responding to God in whatever way seems appropriate based on the review of your day. This might involve asking forgiveness, seeking direction, or praise and thanksgiving.[1] Praying the Prayer of Examen is an outstanding way of focusing your heart on God's work in your life, as well as recognizing and putting into practice your own accountability to him.

Accountability to fellow Christians can occur somewhat casually as you participate in the community of a local church. Your church has certain expectations of its members, and the people of your church probably help you understand what those are and, to a certain extent, hold you accountable for living up to them. Beyond that, it's also helpful for Christians to submit themselves to a more intense accountability relationship with one or two other Christians.

This type of accountability relationship is thoroughly biblical, as evidenced in James 5:13–16:

Is any one of you in trouble? He should pray. Is anyone happy? Let him sing songs of praise. Is any one of you sick? He should call the elders of the church to pray over him and anoint him with oil in the name of the Lord. And the prayer offered in faith will make the sick person well; the Lord will raise him up. If he has sinned, he will be forgiven. Therefore confess your sins to each other and pray for each other so that you may be healed. The prayer of a righteous man is powerful and effective.

The passage showcases the wisdom in letting others shoulder loads with you, both in bad times (in trouble, sick) and in good times (happy). Notice that in the middle of all this load-shouldering, verse 16 implores us to "confess [our] sins to each other and pray for each other so that [we] may be healed." The implication is that we are all in need of healing—physical, mental, emotional, spiritual—and leaning on each other is a biblical way to achieve that healing.

Unlike a physical diet, where your accountability partner is merely helping you keep track of your eating habits, the process of renewing your mind requires someone with whom you're willing to share very intimately about your innermost thought life. For this reason, you'll need to seriously consider several issues before you approach someone about entering an accountability relationship.

QUALITIES OF AN ACCOUNTABILITY PARTNER OR GROUP

Accountability works best one-on-one or in small groups. If you're already involved in a life-giving small group through your church, a group where you have firm relationships with all the participants, each of you might participate in a mind renewal diet and lift each other up every time you meet. However, if you aren't involved in such a group, you'll need to search a little harder for a person who'll be a good fit for you in an accountability relationship.

1. CHOOSE AN ACCOUNTABILITY PARTNER OF THE SAME SEX

This is crucial. You'll be sharing the intimate details of your thought life, and it's simply too easy to allow that intimacy to become inappropriate. (For the sake of our discussion, we're going to use men as examples, but women certainly have the same need for accountability.)

2. CHOOSE A PEER

If possible, establish a peer accountability relationship. This is where each person treats the others as more or less equal in standing or status, rather than one person being considered the teacher, or mentor, or counselor. You're looking for a partner, not a supervisor. It's ideal if your partner or partners are also participating in a mind renewal diet. If they're not, or have already done so, make sure they understand that

> The ancient Romans had a tradition: whenever one of their engineers constructed an arch, as the capstone was hoisted into place, the engineer assumed accountability for his work in the most profound way possible—he stood under the arch.
>
> —Michael Armstrong

their role is not to be a counselor or mentor or the diet police, but to be a supportive, encouraging presence in your life.

3. CHOOSE SOMEONE WHO IS SPIRITUALLY MATURING

Since you're looking for much more than a buddy with whom to talk about the weather or your families, you'll want to approach someone who is growing in his Christian life, someone who's seeking a deeper relationship with God. This person will be:

- Behaviorally focused—he won't tempt you into immoral activities.

- Cognitively clean—he won't pollute your mind with ungodly thoughts.

- Emotionally relevant—he will encourage you to be open and truthful.

- Spiritually renewed—he consistently invests himself in your personal relationship with God.[2]

4. CHOOSE A PERSON WHO IS NONJUDGMENTAL

The last thing that you'll need when you begin sharing with another person about your innermost thoughts is for that person to verbally abuse you for entertaining such thoughts. The mind can be a pretty messy place. The reason you're on the mind renewal diet is that you want to take responsibility for it and clean it up.

It's important that the person you choose be able to accept you for who you are and where you are right now, instead of berating you that you ever let your mind get in such a horrible mess.

5. CHOOSE SOMEONE WHO UNDERSTANDS HIS OWN BROKENNESS

The best way to be sure your accountability partner can listen without being judgmental is to only choose someone who genuinely understands that he is a sinner too; that we all are. It's only when we understand our own brokenness that we can truly minister to others in their brokenness. A person who never wrestles with sin himself (or more accurately, never admits to it) will not make a good accountability partner for you on your thought diet.

6. CHOOSE A PERSON WHO IS TRUSTWORTHY

Since you'll be revealing the truth about yourself and your thought life, you'll want to know your accountability partner can be trusted to maintain confidentiality. Don't be shy about asking the person directly if he is able to maintain your confidence and if he has ever broken a confidence in the past. If so, ask what the circumstances were of his breaking confidence. You can't be too careful when it comes to sharing at this level. A person who is uncomfortable with being asked such questions probably is not the right accountability partner for you.

7. CHOOSE SOMEONE WHO CAN SPEAK THE TRUTH IN LOVE TO YOU

While you need someone who can listen and understand without being judgmental, you're also looking for real accountability, not a pat on the back or a rationalization for your behavior and attitudes. Find a person who you know can look you in the eye and say, "My brother, I love and respect you, but that was wrong."

Even more, find a person that you're willing to hear the truth in love from. In other words, it needs to be a person that you respect and trust.

As you can see, the qualifications for an accountability partner are quite high. You probably won't just stumble across the perfect candidate in the checkout line in the grocery store. In fact, it might take you a while to find the right person. Be patient. This is too important a choice to rush into making a decision. Trust that God will lead you to the right person in his timing.

By the same token, just because it might be hard to find someone, don't use that as an excuse to put off finding someone or to eliminate the practice of accountability

> Two are better than one, because they have a good return for their work: If one falls down, his friend can help him up. But pity the man who falls and has no one to help him up! Also, if two lie down together, they will keep warm. But how can one keep warm alone? Though one may be overpowered, two can defend themselves. A cord of three strands is not quickly broken.
>
> —Ecclesiastes 4:9–12

altogether. As I said at the beginning of the chapter, nothing will help you achieve success with the mind renewal diet like having another person to hold you accountable for sticking with it.

Instead of simply waiting and hoping you'll find someone, ask God to direct you to the person he has for you, then go out and find him. This is another instance where you can claim Mark 11:24—"Whatever you ask for in prayer, believe that you have received it, and it will be yours"—because you can be sure it is God's will for your thought life to align with his Word.

If you are a bit shy about just asking someone to consider meeting with you for this purpose, talk with your pastor or another leader at your church. They will probably be thrilled that you are taking this step and will do whatever they can to help you find the right person to hold you accountable. At the same time, don't select an accountability partner based on your pastor's recommendation alone. It needs to be your choice, because you're the one who's got the most to gain and the most to lose. Once you've found the right person, your pastor or other church leader might even be willing to facilitate an initial meeting and help you establish ground rules and get off to a good start.

Next, let's take a look at the elements of an accountability meeting.

WHAT TO DO WHEN YOU MEET WITH YOUR ACCOUNTABILITY PARTNER

At your first meeting with your accountability partner or group, you'll want to establish a schedule and a few ground rules. For the purposes of this section, we'll assume that the person or people you'll be meeting with will be submitting themselves for accountability too. But the principles and process can work just as well if you're in a one-on-one situation where you're the only one sharing.

ESTABLISH A SCHEDULE AND TIME FRAME

The first item of business at your first meeting should be to decide how often you want (or need) to meet. Maybe you need to get together once a week at the beginning, maybe twice a month. Most important is setting a regular time and place; you can adjust the frequency as you go. Also consider how long the relationship will last. In most cases, rather than agreeing to meet indefinitely, you'll want to establish a specific length for the relationship, like six months or one year. Then, at the end of that period, you can decide whether to re-covenant or go your separate ways.

ESTABLISH GROUND RULES

Accountability partnerships can be pretty serious business, so it's essential that you and your partner or partners agree to maintain confidentiality. This means that what's said in the group stays in the group. Period. There's no outside discussion with spouses or other friends about anything brought up in the meeting unless you have the specific permission of the person who shared the information. You might even want to put your confidentiality covenant in writing and have each person sign it. (For a Sample Accountability Covenant, see Appendix E in the back of this book.)

> The difference between Christian accountability relationships and those based on secular ideas is that the Christian seeks to transform and redeem the entire individual, not simply the harmful behavior (or thought patterns).
>
> —Rob Jackson

Without such a verbal or written covenant—and strict adherence to it—your accountability partnership cannot last.

BEGIN WITH PRAYER

Always. It's easy to forget this step, so make sure you discipline yourself to include God in your meeting from the very beginning by praying for his presence, wisdom, mercy, and guidance during the meeting. Ask God to give each of you the courage to be honest with him and with each other. Pray for discernment in what questions to ask each other and for love and grace to be expressed.

SHARE A BRIEF SUMMARY

After praying together, give each person an opportunity to share briefly (no more than five minutes) about how he's been doing with keeping his mind healthy and what he's been struggling with most. As a group, you might even decide to ask each person to write out his summary ahead of time and read it to the group. This will encourage each person to think ahead of time about what to share at the meeting. By preparing for the meeting, each person can be sure to get the most out of the meeting.

SHARE MORE DEEPLY

Once each person has had a chance to share a brief summary, then you'll choose a person to go first in sharing more deeply about their thought life. Accountability partners can ask specific questions, like those found in Appendix F, to encourage the person to dig more deeply. Start by asking questions that feel safer and less probing, such as "Tell us more about how your thought life has been this week?" or "Where have you been experiencing a lot of success in your thinking this week?" Gradually, as the person becomes more comfortable sharing, progress into the more challenging questions.

> And let us consider how we may spur one another on toward love and good deeds. Let us not give up meeting together, as some are in the habit of doing, but let us encourage one another—and all the more as you see the Day approaching.
>
> —Hebrews 10:24–25

For newer accountability partnerships, you might not dig as deeply in your first few meetings while you're still getting to know one another and building trust so that each of you feels safe. Make sure that you go at a pace that feels comfortable to each person and that you don't push anyone to share too much too quickly. Let each person decide how quickly to open up and share more. You can certainly invite or encourage someone to share more deeply, but be sure that no one feels required to do more than is comfortable. Sometimes it takes patience to allow a person to develop enough trust to share at the level he needs to share, but really that is the only way to develop a strong, healthy accountability relationship.

As you develop trust in your accountability partner or group, give them permission to ask you about anything, no matter how personal it may seem to you. There should be no topic off-limits, whether it's your marriage, your habits, your finances, the way you treat other people, the way you interact with the opposite sex, your innermost thoughts about all those things—nothing is sacred when it comes to your accountability partner. For example, "How much time did you spend watching TV this week?" "How did that compare to what you'd scheduled?" "What has God shown you about yourself this week?" "What are you doing with that knowledge?"

These types of questions may feel a bit invasive at first, but they are crucial to forging the type of deep relationship that is necessary in accountability. And surprisingly, there is an enormous relief that comes from sharing this type of information with someone. Keeping the answers to these types of questions to yourself tends to lead to an endless cycle of self-doubt and self-recrimination. Getting it out into the open and hearing that someone else struggles with the same things you do, is extremely affirming and liberating.

The final, most vital, and potentially most painful question to ask is this: "Have you answered all the previous questions truthfully?" It may sound extreme, but accountability without total honesty is no accountability at all.

If you're in a group or partnership where more than one person is submitting themselves for accountability, after the first person wraps up his sharing, give another person a chance to talk in more depth about how their mind renewal diet is going. Continue until everyone has had a chance to share more deeply. If you are in a larger group, you might set up a regular rotation, so that only two or three people share more deeply at each meeting.

END THE MEETING

Once everyone has had a chance to share, you can begin to wrap up the meeting. Thank each person for their honest sharing and for providing their support. Remind one another when and where the next meeting will take place. Commit to praying for one another in the mean time. Then, the final element of your meeting is the same as the first, pray together. Thank God for enabling you to be truthful with each other, thank him for his forgiveness, and ask him to strengthen you and empower you through his Spirit to take your thoughts captive and to live for him in the days ahead.

DON'T FORGET ABOUT CLOSURE

When it's time for your accountability partnership to come to an end, it's possible and even likely that you and others will have some strong feelings. You'll have invested a lot in each other and maybe have even grown very close to each other. Be sure to give yourself time to grieve the end of the accountability relationship. Talk together about what you've enjoyed, what you'll miss, and what your future relationship might look like. Share what you've appreciated about your partner or partners. By working through a process of closure, you'll be much better prepared for the end of the relationship.

Now let's check in with Jake.

JAKE'S PROGRESS

Jake is excited about the prospect of inviting someone else into his thought life. He's also a bit anxious since he's never done it before. But there's something intriguing and motivating about the idea of having a partner help him keep his mind clean. Since Laurie went on the media fast with him and is participating in an overall mind renewal diet, he knows he can rely on her to keep him accountable (and she knows she can rely on him too).

However, he also knows that there are parts of his interior life that would best be discussed with another man, someone who approaches life from the same direction he does. Laurie knows this as well about herself, and so they decide that each of them will turn to a close relationship they have within their church body.

> The highest proof of true friendship is the intimacy that holds nothing back and admits the friend to share our inmost secrets.
> —Andrew Murray

Jake begins to meet with his friend Paul, getting together with him every couple of weeks for coffee and conversation. Astonishingly, though Jake has made great strides in his spiritual life, and therefore in his life in general, he hasn't ever really talked them through with anyone other than his wife. Discussing with Paul, keeping him up to date on the changes taking place within his mind, Jake comes even more alive and begins to see how far he's really come.

He also appreciates the balance Paul brings to the conversation, especially when they discuss things that affect them as men. Of course this applies to areas of sexual temptation, but also to areas of masculinity in general: the responsibility of being a leader in the home, the everyday pressures of their lives, and other things. The partnership with Paul is a very life-giving relationship for Jake.

Jake's also begun talking with a few people at work, especially one coworker who attends a different church than Jake. While they agree on the basics of their faith, they've recently had interesting discussions on the political role of Christians in the world today. Should Christians be politically active or shouldn't they? Jake had his mind made up—until he began talking with this fellow, who had a different opinion. After hearing what his coworker had to say, Jake began to reconsider his own opinions. He turned to the Bible and discovered a passage that validated what he had already decided. But the search and the give-and-take with his coworker helped him solidify his belief, and ultimately that relationship spurred him on to higher thinking, which we'll discuss more in a later chapter.

One other thing that really contributed to Jake's turnaround, which I mentioned before, is the next practice for us to focus on in the mind renewal process—prayer.

LOCK IT DOWN

Now complete these five exercises to apply what you learned in this chapter.

1. Set aside fifteen minutes each day for one week to examine your heart in the presence of God through prayer, using the pattern laid out in this chapter. Ask God to reveal to you where you have succeeded and where you need to focus more effort and energy.

2. Identify two or three people that you already know who might make a suitable accountability partner for you. If you don't know anyone who might fit the bill, ask a pastor or other church leader to help you develop such a list. Begin praying for each person on your list on a daily basis and ask God for his guidance in choosing an accountability partner, either one that's on your list or someone you haven't yet thought of or even met.

3. Decide how you will approach the person you want to ask about being your accountability partner. Do you want to talk to the person by e-mail, on the phone, or in person? Most often, it works well to use e-mail or phone to set up a face-to-face meeting. Set yourself a deadline for making that contact. Be prepared that the first person you contact

may not end up being your accountability partner for one reason or another.

4. Prepare well for your first accountability meeting. Know what you will say to your potential partner about what you're hoping to accomplish and what you're hoping the person might do to help you. Consider beforehand about how often you'd like to meet, and maybe even when and where. Keep in mind, though, that the more flexible you can be in your meeting time and place, the easier it will be to find a time that works for both of you. Know ahead of time what your options are.

5. After you've met with your accountability partner a few times, take some time to review how your meetings are going. What is working well? What's not working as well? What changes might you make to help your meetings be more beneficial? Get your partner's input as well. Then discuss what, if any, changes you'd like to make to your meeting arrangement.

Practice 7

Cultivate an
Attitude of Prayer

FOCUS

a lifestyle of

prayer keeps

the mind

healthy

Over the past twenty-five years, I have prayed the Lord's Prayer on a daily basis. It was not a prayer our Lord needed to pray for his own benefit. Rather, he prayed it as a model for all believers. I have found that uttering this prayer to God on a daily basis brings incredible peace at the times when I most need it.

You've probably often heard prayer described as talking to God. And this is very true, although I prefer to call it talking *with* God. Saying that prayer is talking to God makes it one-sided and one-dimensional—it becomes more about unloading a stream of words in God's direction than about talking and listening. And the listening can be the most important part of prayer.

> Prayer is nothing else than being on terms of friendship with God.
> —Teresa of Ávila

When we pray, we are choosing to take advantage of an open line of communication with the Creator of the universe. Look around you. Look out the window, up at the sky. Spend just a few moments taking in the wonders of all that God created: trees, insects, animals, flowers, the eyes of a loved one, the moon, the sun, the coffee bean. What a marvelous, miraculous, incredible, indescribable God! And he wants to spend time talking with us! Wouldn't we be foolish not to listen once in a while?

Prayer is an important part of your life in Christ for so many reasons, not the least of which is renewing your mind. In fact, prayer is such a key component of the mind renewal diet that I hope you've been practicing it throughout your detoxification process, as you've been developing healthy thinking, and as you sought out a life-giving accountability relationship. That's why I've suggested it numerous times in the Lock It Down section at the end of each chapter as a way to apply the principles you're learning. I hope that prayer infuses every part of your life; not just your mind. Now, we want to focus on prayer itself and how it energizes and empowers you for the renewal of your mind.

LEARNING FROM THE LORD'S PRAYER

You may already have a fairly solid concept of the essence of prayer. Still, many of us need to learn how to do it and then run with it. Fortunately, the Bible is quite specific about this very issue. We find our instructions from Jesus himself in Matthew 6:5–15:

> And when you pray, do not be like the hypocrites, for they love to pray standing in the synagogues and on the street corners to be seen by men. I tell you the truth, they

have received their reward in full. But when you pray, go into your room, close the door and pray to your Father, who is unseen. Then your Father, who sees what is done in secret, will reward you. And when you pray, do not keep on babbling like pagans, for they think they will be heard because of their many words. Do not be like them, for your Father knows what you need before you ask him.

● ● ● ROADBLOCKS TO EFFECTIVE PRAYER

Unconfessed Sin: "If I had cherished sin in my heart, the Lord would not have listened" (Ps. 66:18).

Selfish Motives: "When you ask, you do not receive, because you ask with wrong motives, that you may spend what you get on your pleasures" (James 4:3).

Pride: "God opposes the proud but gives grace to the humble" (James 4:6).

Doubt: "When he asks, he must believe and not doubt, because he who doubts is like a wave of the sea, blown and tossed by the wind. That man should not think he will receive anything from the Lord" (James 1:6–7).

Stinginess: "If a man shuts his ears to the cry of the poor, he too will cry out and not be answered" (Prov. 21:13).

Unforgiveness: "For if you forgive men when they sin against you, your heavenly Father will also forgive you. But if you do not forgive men their sins, your Father will not forgive your sins" (Matt. 6:14–15).

This, then, is how you should pray: "Our Father in heaven, hallowed be your name, your kingdom come, your will be done on earth as it is in heaven. Give us today our daily bread. Forgive us our debts, as we also have forgiven our debtors. And lead us not into temptation, but deliver us from the evil one." For if you forgive men when they sin against you, your heavenly Father will also forgive you. But if you do not forgive men their sins, your Father will not forgive your sins.

There is so much to learn in these two paragraphs. There is a rich vein of teaching to be mined for our mind renewal diet, not to mention our broader spiritual lives. The first paragraph is an admonishment about the parameters of prayer. Jesus warns about the attitude behind our prayers, telling us that people who pray as part of a big show or people who go on and on and on while they pray are missing the point.

When people stand out on the street corners to be seen by men while they pray, we must question the motivation behind their prayers. Are they really praying to communicate with God, or are they praying to look like they're communicating with God? Are they seeking an audience with the Almighty or are they seeking an audience with the world, hoping those around them will look up in awe at the way they pray? In prayer, we should always be impressed with God, not ourselves.

When people keep on babbling like pagans, using many words in their prayers, what is their motivation? Are they really trying to communicate with God, or are they trying to impress him (or us) with their brilliant language? Are they turning to their Creator in due submission to his mighty power, or are they trying to use verbal puffery to convince God to act on their behalf? Is it about God's will being done or their own? You don't have to convince God to do what's best for you. He already wants to do that.

> Pray often; for prayer is a shield to the soul, a sacrifice to God, and a scourge for Satan.
>
> —John Bunyan

Prayer is not about trying to influence God or motivate him to act on our behalf. It's not about impressing others. It's about conversing—sharing and listening, understanding God's heart. That's the point.

We cannot judge the hearts of others as they pray; we can only judge our own heart, and here we have a dire warning from Jesus about the nature of our heart as we pray. Perhaps this is why Jesus' example of prayer begins with "our Father in heaven." This very line is an act of submission, like a child acknowledging her own father's parental authority over her. It is a way of making sure our heart is in the right place when we pray.

The next line announces God's holiness and sovereignty: "Hallowed be your name, your kingdom come, your will be done on earth as it is in heaven." When we pray this, we are acknowledging that God's name is holy and that he is in charge of us. He is the king, we are his subjects, and his will is of the utmost importance in our lives.

After setting our hearts in the right place, it's time to offer up our requests to God. We can request provision for our own needs or the needs of others ("give us today our daily bread"), for forgiveness ("forgive us our debts"), and for protection and freedom from sin ("lead us not into temptation"). And notice the reminder to keep our hearts pointed in a godly direction, with an attitude of forgiveness toward others. It's a reminder that we're all on a level playing field, that we're all in need of forgiveness, and if we try to withhold it from others, God will withhold it from us.

Now that we've covered the basics of prayer, let's dig into the different ways we can live out this prayer life.

I've heard a lot of conversational prayers to Father Weejus. You know, "Father Weejus ask that you'd be here tonight, and Weejus hope you'll really bless our time." I've heard a lot of unnecessary "justs" and "reallys" over the years, and inappropriate uses of the subjunctive mood. ("We pray you *would* move your people and you *would* do your will.")

I'm all for conversational prayer. But a lot of it is sloppy, which, I'm afraid, has been bred by too much informality.

Christians didn't always pray like this. For, oh, about 1,950 years, followers of Christ prayed with a great deal of reverence. Augustine prayed in Confessions: "Is there anything in me, O Lord my God, that can contain you? Do even the heaven and the earth, which you have made, and in which you did make me, contain you?"

Conversational? Yes. Informal? No.

—Tony Jones

FOUR KEYS TO EFFECTIVE PRAYER

1. Claim the presence of Christ in our midst, expecting him to actually be present by his Spirit as he promised.
2. Trust him to take charge of us, because he is the Head of the Church.
3. Be completely willing for him to change each one of us as he sees fit.
4. Agree to trust him to bring us into harmony with his Father and thus into heaven's harmony with one another.

—Oliver W. Price

We all know the standard way of praying, a way which many of us practice: kneeling down, praying aloud. We may go someplace private, like our office, but the general pattern for most of the praying population is to assume a specific posture of prayer, to say our piece, and then follow it with "Amen" and go on our way.

Or, perhaps you're one of the many people who prays without saying a word out loud. Many of us practice this type of thought prayer instead of speaking our prayer, or in addition to it. Thought prayers are essential to the mind renewal diet and are a great way to invite God into your mind and allow him to rule and reign there.

In a sense, we need to keep our hearts hot. To prevent soot buildup in a chimney, many wood stove owners in days gone by would keep their stove hot. The same principle applies to your heart, which will then influence your mind. Keep your heart hot by pursuing God on a regular basis. When you commune with him in prayer, you're doing just that. Take time alone with God to kindle your flame, stir the coals of your heart, and let his glory fill you. You'll find that your mind is free of soot such as pride, envy, jealousy, greed, lust, and the like.

ESTABLISHING A LIFESTYLE OF PRAYER

In my time as a pastor, I've identified six different components that have helped make prayer a way of life for me.

1. PRAY DAILY

Prayer is how we connect with our Source of strength, so it only makes sense to tap into that strength on a regular, daily basis.

2. PRAY EARLY

When you make time to pray every day, try to make that time in the early part of the day. Personally, I pray first thing every day before I do anything else. It's a surefire way to get my time with God with no worries that I will be invaded by phone calls, unexpected visitors, and other interruptions.

3. PRAY UP

I also make my prayers focused on God instead of myself. It's so easy to pray about myself, but that throws my perspective out of whack. Instead, I pray up. I praise and glorify God, and I find myself lifted up because of it.

4. PRAY OUT

In addition to praying upward, I pray out and pray for the needs of other people along with my own needs. I don't limit my prayers to myself; I lift up others all the time, and find myself invigorated as a result.

5. PRAY IN FAITH

Another important component in prayer is the audacity to trust God's bigness. He's a great God, and he can do great things! There is no need too great to take to our loving Father, and there is no need too small. He encompasses them all and he cares about them all. Trust God on every level and you'll be refreshed to see him move in your life in both big and small ways.

6. PRAY ALWAYS

The final component of a lifestyle of prayer is having a constantly open line of communication with God. Having an attitude of prayer "without ceasing," as Paul mentioned in 1 Thessalonians 5:17 (KJV), is like having God constantly updating you, like having full signal bars on your cell phone. You're always ready to receive; you're never in a low signal area. I'm not saying that you need to spend your life in constant prayer. I'm saying you need to have an open heart toward God at all times—always ready to pray, always ready to listen.

A regular time of prayer—of having a thought conversation with God—is a vital part of a healthy thought life. By conversing with God mentally, you are not only supporting all the work you've put into your detoxification and your right thinking, you're also appealing to God for help to keep you on the right thought track.

Our Father, you called us and saved us in order to make us like your Son, our Lord Jesus Christ. Change us, day by day, by the work of your Holy Spirit so that we may grow more like him in all that we think and say and do, to his glory. Amen.

—Søren Kierkegaard

But having a thought conversation with God doesn't mean you have to sit in a dark room, eyes closed, concentrating all your energies on hearing from the Almighty. There are many ways to engage God mentally, including writing your prayers, reading them, speaking them in one or two words under your breath, and praying for others.

TYPES OF PRAYER

There's something substantial that comes from writing, something that makes your thoughts seem more forceful, as if putting them to paper has given them more weight. Perhaps it's the finality of the process; the knowledge that, while your thoughts are fleeting, the written word is permanent. It's difficult—if not impossible—to page through old thoughts in your mind; paging through notes you've written down, even if they're only thoughts scribbled on scrap paper, is an entirely different story.

All of which are good reasons to consider writing out some of your prayers to God. Don't worry about editing them as you write. Don't bother with proper punctuation or grammar. Just get out a pen or pencil, a piece of paper or a notebook, and begin to pour your heart out to God right there on the paper. Perhaps you prefer a keyboard and computer screen, which is perfectly okay too. If you feel like God is saying something back to you, write it down—it's good to have a record of both sides of the conversation the best that you can understand it.

You may want to try writing out your prayer as a letter to God. It's a great way to unburden your heart before him, or to thank him for something he's done in your life, or just to let him know how you feel about him. And you don't need to trouble yourself with finding a stamp or envelope!

Another way to pray is to open the Bible and read the words you find there as a prayer. It can be the Lord's Prayer, which I mentioned earlier in the chapter, or another time when Jesus spoke or preached, or you can insert yourself into the text of a verse or passage, like this example from Ephesians 1:17–21:

I keep asking that [you,] the God of our Lord Jesus Christ, the glorious Father, may give [me] the Spirit of wisdom and revelation, so that [I] may know [you] better. I pray also that the eyes of [my] heart may be enlightened in order that [I] may know the hope to which [you have] called [me], the riches of [your] glorious inheritance in the saints, and [your] incomparably great power for us who believe. That power is like the working of [your] mighty strength, which [you] exerted in Christ when [you] raised him from the dead and seated him at his right hand in the heavenly realms, far above all rule and authority, power and dominion, and every title that can be given, not only in the present age but also in the one to come.

Of course, it's not good to get in the habit of changing Scripture around on a whim, but as you can see here, all I did was change this prayer from one prayed by the apostle Paul about the Ephesian church, to one prayed by myself directly to God. I made it personal by changing a few subjects and objects in some of the sentences, but not changing a hair of the intent.

If you have trouble finding passages in the Bible to pray over yourself, you might look into obtaining a book of thematically arranged Scripture references and quotes. You can find these at almost any Christian bookstore or on book-selling Web sites.

They are usually indexed by need, with categories like healing, provision, security, faith, trust, and so on. You simply look for the theme that concerns you and find a host of different Scriptures or references that apply to that need. You are then armed with the Bible's counsel about those areas, able to pray according to those Scriptures, or to look them up and get a deeper understanding of their context.

While you're at the Christian bookstore or surfing a book-selling Web site, you can also check into purchasing a book of prayers. Many godly men and women throughout history have written incredibly beautiful and heartfelt prayers, and oftentimes you can find these prayers collected in one volume. These are good to pull out when you just don't know what to say in your prayers or how to pray about a specific topic.

Another source for prayer help is the Internet, which is now replete with prayer resources, including complete biblical texts online at places like www.bible.com or www.biblegateway.com. You can often find subject indices and can search a variety of translations over the Internet for a specific passage or key word. Personally, I find it difficult to pray while sitting at my computer's keyboard, but it might suit you perfectly.

Another method of prayer that I find effective is called breath prayer. These are simple, one-sentence prayers you say—in rhythm with your inhale and exhale—throughout the day, or just as you think of praying. They are effective when you are in a situation where you can't retire to a quiet, isolated place to pray. Like when you're on your way into a business meeting or when you're running late to drop the kids off at school. Breath prayers are a great way to acknowledge God's lordship and presence in that moment, like a child taking a break from playing outside to give his dad a hug, then going back to the swings.

You don't have to be eloquent. You don't have to create Shakespearean prose when you pray a breath prayer (or any prayer for that matter). It can be as simple as "Help me, Lord!" or "Thanks for this day." Again, as Jesus said, it's not about babbling on and on—it's about focusing your heart, even for a brief moment, on the God of all creation.

One final idea about prayer: I've talked a lot about ways to pray for yourself, which is always going to be a smart thing to do. But don't forget to pray for other people as well. Use all these different methods of

O God, early in the
morning I cry to you.
Help me to pray
And to concentrate my
thoughts on you:
I cannot do this alone.
In me there is darkness,
But with you there is light;
I am lonely, but you do not
leave me;
I am feeble in heart, but with
you there is help;
I am restless, but with you
there is peace.
In me there is bitterness, but
with you there is patience;
I do not understand your ways,
But you know the way for me . . .
Restore me to liberty,
And enable me to live now
That I may answer before you
and before me.
Lord, whatever this day
may bring,
Your name be praised.

—Dietrich Bonhoeffer

prayer to lift up those around you, or maybe even people you don't know.

Pray for your children and grandchildren, that they will have a future according to God's plan for their lives. Pray for your spouse, that he or she will draw closer to God and therefore closer to you. Pray for the president to exercise wisdom in guiding the country. Pray for your boss or coworkers, even the ones you don't like—especially for the ones you don't like. When you pray for those people who are difficult to love, you begin to find it easier to love them. It's a great way to change the way you think about the world around you.

You get the idea. These are only suggestions, and I'm sure your mind is brimming with possibilities of other people you could be praying for. It could be your landlord, an estranged family member, the person who just cut you off in traffic, or the barista who makes your half-caf soy vanilla latte every morning. There is a world of over six billion people out there, and we all could use someone in our corner, praying for us.

JAKE'S PROGRESS

Jake spent a lot of time in prayer during his detoxification process, but much of that time was just talking to God as he drove to work. Now Jake wants to take his prayer life to the next level, especially regarding his common, recurring concern about provision for his family, so he went to the Bible Gateway Web site and did a topical search on *faith*. There he was met with almost one hundred different verses about the topic. He printed them out, and now spends a little time each morning looking up a different one, reading what it says, and praying it over himself and his family.

For quite some time, Jake has had a strained relationship with his stepfather, the man his mother married after Jake's father passed away. It just hasn't been the same for Jake, and he's had difficulty allowing this man—who is assuredly not his father—into his life. It isn't so much that he doesn't approve of the marriage. His mother was free to marry whomever she wished. Still, he doesn't feel right about it in his spirit, for whatever reason. It has gotten to the point that Jake and his wife and children never see his mother and stepfather anymore, and they don't even talk about them. It's just too uncomfortable for everyone involved.

So Jake felt prompted by God to begin to pray for his stepfather. He has decided to write a letter to God about his feelings, expecting it to be a page or two long. Four pages later, he finishes it off, astonished at all that came out as he wrote. He shares the letter with his wife, and suddenly it's a little easier to talk about the situation.

Jake decides to investigate a book of family prayers that might help him learn how to pray for his stepfather. In consulting that book, he finds a few wonderfully worded prayers that he begins to pray over his stepfather every now and then, just as he thinks of it. As the days pass, he notices his attitude toward his stepfather has begun to change.

Before he began praying in earnest about his stepfather, Jake would recoil inside his heart when he would think of the man. Now, though he still carries that feeling in his spirit, the feeling that says something isn't quite right, he carries a much better heart attitude toward his stepfather. Now he doesn't recoil; he stands firm and loves him as best he can. He is beginning to give the entire situation over to God and is eager to see how it might resolve.

And this is just one instance of the way prayer is changing Jake's life. He and his wife are praying together on a regular basis and are growing closer to each other as they grow closer to God. He's noticing that his first response when talking to his children is to pray for them if they have questions or sustain those minor injuries children are so prone to.

On the other hand, since Jake finished his detoxification process, he's started to slip in his media intake, and he's finding that he isn't nearly as focused in his relationship with God as he was during his media fast. He needs to move on to the next step in the mind renewal diet: he needs to regulate what he lets into his mind.

LOCK IT DOWN

Now complete these five exercises to apply what you learned in this chapter.

1. Many have considered the book of Psalms in the Old Testament to be a school of prayer. Commit to reading a psalm a day for the next thirty days. Take notes on what you learn about prayer from your reading. Does anything surprise you? What do you find in the Psalms to emulate in your own prayer life?

2. Create a personal prayer list, either handwritten or on your computer or other electronic device. Use it as a reminder to pray daily and to thank God for his answers to your prayers.

3. If you're feeling a bit overwhelmed by the thought of praying regularly, and you're not quite sure where to start or what to say, consider using the ACTS method of prayer:

   - **Adoration:** Tell God who he is and what he's done. (He already knows, of course, but praising him helps us to focus on him and remember the greatness of our Heavenly Father.)

- **Confession:** Take time to acknowledge and repent of your sins and failures to God, turning away from wrongdoing and toward right and holy living and thinking.

- **Thanksgiving:** Express gratitude to the Lord for his forgiveness, for his faithfulness, and for all the blessings he's given you.

- **Supplication:** Ask God to meet the needs of your family and friends, your coworkers, your leaders, those who minister in other parts of the world, and so forth.

4. Which of the steps to establishing a lifestyle of prayer (pray daily, early, up, out, in faith, always) is most difficult for you? Ask God to bring that step to mind each day and to help you make that step a permanent part of your prayer life.

5. Develop a plan for prayer that you think you can actually implement and be faithful to in your daily life. It doesn't have to be a grand scheme or require huge amounts of time. Just start with a simple plan that involves conversing with God on a daily basis.

Practice 8

Stretch Your Thinking

FOCUS

elevate your

mind by expanding,

evaluating, and

analyzing its intake

While I was a college student, I worked with John C. Maxwell, who is now one of the leading authors and speakers on the topic of leadership. Later, I would serve with him as vice president of INJOY, a company he created to help develop Christian leaders. People often ask me what it was like working with him. I always respond, "He stretched me beyond belief." John taught me to think right!

All the previous mind renewal practices have guided you on the pathway to a healthy mind: *detoxification* rids your mind of built-up negativity; *adjusting your view of yourself* and seeing yourself the way God sees you restores your perspective and helps you to see your value; *taking control of your media intake* helps you to limit unhealthy influences; *finding a Barnabas* or two keeps you from becoming discouraged and giving up; *accountability* keeps you pointed in the right direction; and *prayer* focuses your attention on God instead of on yourself.

These practices are all essential for a lifestyle of healthy thinking. But there's one more behavior that you need to engage in to maintain your health: exercise. While a healthy diet is crucial for maintaining a healthy body, exercise is the key factor that pushes our body past its natural limits and makes us stronger, healthier, and more resilient.

Ask any physician what you need to do to maintain a healthy lifestyle, and ninety-nine times out of a hundred the doctor will say, "Eat right and exercise." In the same way, your mind needs exercise as much as it needs healthy input. The mind renewal diet is not just about keeping out the wrong kinds of thinking; it's also about learning how to strengthen our minds by incorporating higher thinking.

HIGHER THINKING 101

Psychologists and educators have written a lot of articles and books about higher thinking, especially since the 1950s, when Benjamin Bloom, a professor at the University of Chicago, created the "Taxonomy of Educational Objectives." What soon came to be known as "Bloom's Taxonomy" describes and defines how thinking and learning develop through stages in the mind of a person. Think of the stages described below as a sort of pyramid, beginning with the bottom. (Or for a more thorough look, see Appendix G.)

- **Remember:** Can you define, duplicate, list, memorize, recall, repeat, or reproduce information?

- **Understand:** Can you classify, describe, discuss, explain, identify, locate, recognize, report, select, translate, or paraphrase information?

- **Apply:** Can you use the information to demonstrate, dramatize, illustrate, or interpret other information?

- **Analyze:** Can you appraise, compare, contrast, criticize, examine, or question different parts of the information?

- **Evaluate:** Can you use the information to defend or support a decision?

- **Create:** Can you use the information to construct, design, or develop something new?[1]

> Your higher thinking system activates whenever you meet up with information or challenges whose meanings or solutions are not immediately obvious.
>
> —Mel Levine

Though Bloom applied his theories specifically to education, let's see how they apply to everyday life, on your drive to work, for example.

When you get in your car to drive to work, you *remember* significant information: where to put the key, how to engage the transmission, all the mechanics of driving, traffic laws, the route to work, and so forth. You then show that you *understand* the information by recognizing which driving skills you need to use and which traffic laws are relevant to your commute. Next you *apply* that information by actually driving and obeying signs and stoplights as you go.

Now, imagine that a driver changes lanes so that you have to react to avoid an accident. In reacting, you *apply* to the situation knowledge and skill from your storehouse of driving experience so that you hit the brakes to avoid a collision. Once your heart rate returns to normal, you can *analyze* what happened: did the person really cut you off or did you perceive danger where there was none? What was your mind focused on in the moments before the incident? Were there other options available to you for avoiding an accident? What would have happened if you had chosen a different option?

Nurture your mind with great thoughts, for you will never go any higher than you think.

—Benjamin Disraeli

Then, armed with your own analysis, you can *evaluate* your response to the near accident: perhaps you would say that you were already stressed and a little distracted when the driver pulled in front of you. The other person cut it too close, but you also overreacted because you weren't paying careful attention. While the other person should have been less reckless, you too could have been more careful. Based on your self-evaluation, you may or may not choose to *create* a new approach to driving when you're feeling stressed.

This entire process of higher thinking can happen in just a few moments, as in the above example, or over a significant period of time, such as when you are mulling over a significant decision like taking a new job or buying a new house. The reason it works in our scenario is because you've trained yourself to drive skillfully through education and experience.

Likewise, you can train your mind through education and experience to think skillfully in any area of life.

LOOK FOR PATTERNS

One of the first steps to improving your higher thinking skills is to learn to identify patterns. Some of you may remember taking various standardized tests in school that asked you to find the pattern in a series of numbers, words, or symbols. There's a reason they ask those questions. It's because the ability to identify patterns is one of the key skills that's necessary for learning to think at a higher level.

> A man is what he thinks about all day long.
> —Ralph Waldo Emerson

Have you ever known someone who seems to make the same mistake over and over again? Oh, they don't make the exact same mistake twice. They vary it up each time, but they make similar mistakes repeatedly and never seem to understand that's what they're doing. For example, in the morning he dutifully makes his lunch to take with him to work and then leaves it on the kitchen counter on his way out the door. At work that day, he turns in a project he's been working on for weeks, only to learn that he's left out a critical component his supervisor had asked for. On the way home that evening, he stops to pick up flowers for his wife. She appreciates the flowers, but wonders why he didn't also pick up the eggs and flour she'd asked him about.

The man in the above example might look at his three mistakes as completely unrelated, but a thinking person will wonder if there's a connection or a pattern. What pattern do you see? Perhaps it's simply forgetfulness and he needs to carry a notepad with him so that he can write down important bits of information. Maybe he needs to learn to listen better so that he actually hears his supervisor's instructions or his wife's requests. It could be that he's distracted by too many priorities or too much stress and he needs to simplify his life so that he can focus on what's most important. Or maybe something else entirely different is going on. What's important is the ability to recognize that there might be a pattern there. Then you can begin to understand what it might mean and what you might need to do about it.

> Christian discernment means looking at and listening to our mediated culture with the eyes and ears of Christ. We are asked to see truly and hear clearly the sights and sounds of media so that we may know what values and meanings are informing our culture. But it is difficult to see and hear in a world filled with noise, noise that we take for granted. We tend to become conscious of the media only occasionally.
>
> —James McDonnell

> Once we discard the illusion that the mass media offer us an objective, transparent view of reality, we can begin to have confidence in our own perceptions and judgments.
>
> —James McDonnell

The ability to identify patterns is useful for many different reasons. Not only can it help you learn to stop making the same mistake repeatedly, it can also help you make good decisions more quickly. Great leaders, when faced with an important decision, are able to see how the decision might be similar to other decisions they've needed to make in the past. They can then benefit from their past experiences, from what went well and what didn't go so well, and use that information to make a good decision in the present. If wisdom involves learning from experience, then one can only become wise by learning to identify patterns.

THINK CRITICALLY

Another step to improving your higher thinking skills is to learn to think critically. No, I didn't say to be critical or criticize people, but develop and use your critical thinking skills. Thinking critically means to examine and test what you hear or read to learn if it really is the truth, rather than simply taking it on someone else's word. Such examination is important even if the information comes from a person you respect or consider an authority, and even more so if you're not sure what kind of credentials are there to back up the statement. Remember that even the wisest and smartest people are dead wrong a certain percentage of the time. So put out of your mind the thought that it's disrespectful to think critically about what other people tell you. It's absolutely essential. And you can question or challenge another person's assertion with the utmost respect.

The essence behind thinking critically is, whenever you hear or read an assertion or truth claim, examine the foundation of the assertion. What data are they using to support their conclusion? If there's not solid data, then you've got a theory or hypothesis, not an absolute truth. Some theories turn out to be true. Many more don't. Most often, people base their suggestions or arguments on their thinking about their own experience or on what they've heard from people they trust. The point behind critical thinking is to be reasonably sure that what you're hearing or reading has a substantial basis in reality before you accept it as truth. If it can't be substantiated, then call it what it is—a hypothesis or a proposal—but don't uncritically accept it as truth.

There's no way to estimate how many unsubstantiated claims we are subjected to on a daily basis in the media alone, not to mention in casual conversations with friends and colleagues. We simply cannot believe everything we read or hear, or even most of it. That's one reason this thought diet is so beneficial.

HIGHER THINKING AND RENEWING YOUR MIND

When you take in mass media, are you a passive observer (simply absorbing whatever is given to you), or do you mull it over and really think about it as you take it in? When you watch a movie, do you stare passively at the screen, or do you wrestle with the content and meaning of the film? Do you ask yourself what messages the media is intending to convey, or are you a sideline participant?

There is an agenda behind every word, image, and sound you experience in mass media. By using the word *agenda*, I run the risk of sounding like a conspiracy theorist, which I'm most definitely not. But the word is intentionally strong because I want you to understand that people and organizations pay a lot of money to transmit to you every word, image, and sound you experience in the media. The reason they're willing to spend the money to transmit the media is because they want you to get their message. Now don't hear what I'm not saying. I don't mean that every television or radio program, every piece of music or every book and magazine article has a negative or harmful message. I simply mean that every tiny bit of media was created to achieve two purposes: to turn a profit, and to convey some sort of message.

These messages range in terms of gravity from "Laugh at this bit of insanity!" to "Do your part to end this humanitarian crisis!" and include all points in between. A half hour sitcom may simply aim to entertain you long enough for all of those who work on it to pay the bills. On the other hand, a ten-thousand-word lead story in *Time* magazine may hope to spur you to action on whatever cause happens to be in the headlines. The message of most advertising is "Buy this product or service!" The message of most athletic events is "Enjoy this competition vicariously by making yourself a small part of it."

> My mind rebels at stagnation. Give me problems, give me work, give me the most abstruse cryptogram, or the most intricate analysis, and I am in my own proper atmosphere. But I abhor the dull routine of existence. I crave for mental exaltation.
>
> —Sir Arthur Conan Doyle

Are you aware of such messages in the media you consume? Do you seek them out when you watch television or go to the movie theater? Do you look for them between the lines in the books you read or magazine articles you peruse? Do you hear them mixed into the music you listen to? An important skill in higher thinking is the ability to see and evaluate the agenda or message behind a communication. Seeking out these messages is a key step in thinking analytically and thus bringing higher thinking into your mind renewal process.

SEE WHAT OTHERS MISS

Another way to apply higher thinking is to seek and find the spiritual element in the world around you. Just about everything in this life has a spiritual parallel—that's why pastors like me are always able to come up with sermon illustrations and object lessons! God has infused his creation with his own personality, with bits of himself, so it stands to reason that we can examine creation to find those fingerprints, and therefore learn more about its Creator.

A glance at a tree can turn into a magnificent revelation when we learn that the deeper the tree's roots go into the ground, the more it can withstand stormy, windy weather. A visit to the mountains can cause us to ponder the severe tonnage of rock present there, and make real the subsequent power that lies in Jesus' words in Matthew 17:20: "If you have faith as small as a mustard seed, you can say to this mountain, 'Move from here to there' and it will move. Nothing will be impossible for you."

God's messages are literally everywhere, even in the miracle of the air we breathe. We need oxygen to survive, but the air we take in is not pure oxygen—it's actually mostly nitrogen. Too much oxygen affects our minds and bodies and causes passivity, but the air around us has the perfect amount of oxygen to sustain us without affecting us mentally or physically. God has set up the air around us in

> The whole idea of motivation is a trap. Forget motivation. Just do it. Exercise, lose weight, test your blood sugar, or whatever. Do it without motivation. And then, guess what? After you start doing the right thing, that's when the motivation comes and makes it easy for you to keep on doing it.
>
> —John C. Maxwell

perfect balance, giving us exactly what we need. It's a constant reminder of his provision in other areas of our lives.

Pray that God will reveal these types of spiritual parallels to you. Start to look for them in the mass media you consume. A friend of mine was moved to tears when she watched a scene in *Titanic* where Jack (Leonardo DiCaprio) covers Rose's (Kate Winslet) eyes and has her climb onto the rail at the bow of the ship. He asks, "Do you trust me?" and when she says yes, he removes his hands. With her arms out and the wind blowing through her hair, Rose takes in the vastness of the ocean and the thrill of standing above it all. My friend saw that as a picture of God's work in our lives. We so often want to see where we're going, what's around the next corner, but God simply asks, "Do you trust me?" When we learn to say yes, he takes us to new heights in our relationship with him that allow us to trust him even further.

Once you open your eyes to such messages, you'll constantly discover fresh ones in new and unexpected places.

EXPAND YOUR THINKING

Another way to elevate the functioning of your mind is to intentionally increase the overall quality of the mass media you consume.

BOOKS

If you are an avid reader, check out a few literary classics from your local library. There's nothing wrong with occasionally reading a book that has no agenda other than to entertain you, but challenge yourself with something of a higher caliber. If the thought of reading *Moby Dick* or *War and Peace* makes your palms sweat, consider starting with short stories. Many of the great writers of the past and present wrote both novels and short stories. While you may not be ready for full-length classic novels, you can ease your way into them through short stories. You might also want to start with stories you know. For example, Charles Dickens' *A Christmas Carol* is less than one hundred pages, and you probably already know the plot! One other idea is to check out a "best of" or daily reading type of book to introduce yourself to great writers. (Hey, even a daily tear-off calendar with quotes from great writers is a start.) The worst that can happen is that you get bored with the book and send it back to the library largely unread.

MOVIES

Are you a movie fan? Look into some independent motion pictures that fall outside the standard Hollywood blockbuster motif (being careful, of course, to consider the overall content of the movie in question). Engage your mind with film classics or even family safe, subtitled foreign films that will help you see the world from a different perspective.

MUSIC

What about music? Instead of consuming the standard pop music that comprises Top 40 lists, or listening repeatedly to songs from your youth, seek out music that will broaden your horizons. Discover the classic composers or jazz legends. Many local libraries have compilation CDs filled with music from other countries; check them out. Learn about musical history in this country or in other countries and explore the musical and cultural landscape of another civilization.

> Such as are your habitual thoughts, such also will be the character of your mind; for the soul is dyed by the thoughts.
>
> —Marcus Aurelius

I hope you're getting the idea. You need to be intentional about your mass media consumption if you are going to think on a higher level. Take Jake, for example.

JAKE'S PROGRESS

Jake's never been much of a reader, but he enjoyed the Narnia stories as a child, so he decided to reread them to see what C. S. Lewis had to say about God. He had remembered them as entertaining stories, but reading them as an adult, he's discovered many new perspectives on God that he hadn't noticed in his youth.

This led him to look into another C. S. Lewis classic he had always meant to read, *Mere Christianity*. He bought an inexpensive paperback edition from the bookstore down the street from his house and began to thumb through it. It was difficult at first to get into the flow of Lewis's writing, but soon he adjusted to the rhythms and word choice of a British man writing in the year 1943 and even learned to appreciate his style. It took him a little while, but he finished it and found his mind curiously expanded.

Having found *Mere Christianity* enjoyable and profitable, Jake decides to go full bore into Christian classics and obtains *The Imitation of Christ* by Thomas à Kempis, a text that has been a staple in Christianity for almost six hundred years. He slogs his way through the first twenty pages or so, then decides he isn't quite ready for it yet, so he sets it back on his bookshelf with the intent of building up to it.

Jake realizes that this mental exercise of higher thinking is going to be a lifelong pursuit. He hopes that, at some point in his life, he will be at a stage where he can read something like *The Imitation of Christ* without balking at the concepts or the way it is written. He is in this for life, and his next book purchase will take him a step closer to a stronger, healthier mind and a closer relationship with God.

LOCK IT DOWN

Now complete these five exercises to apply what you learned in this chapter.

1. Journal your answers to the following questions: Which of the higher thinking skills discussed in this chapter are skills that you use regularly? Give examples of situations in which they have benefited you. Which higher thinking skills do you need to work on and use more often? How do you think doing so might make a difference in your life?

2. Make it a point to find three opportunities in the next week to exercise your critical thinking skills where a person, either in the media or in person, makes a statement as truth without providing supporting data or argument. Dig deeper to find out how well substantiated the claim is. Then, think about what you learned about critical thinking from the exercise.

3. Watch one of your favorite movies this week. Analyze it and try to determine what message or messages the director wanted to communicate. Is the show an accurate representation of the slice of life it's portraying? Why or why not?

4. Ask God to help you to see him, maybe an aspect of his character, in an unexpected place this week. Then keep your eyes open and watch for him.

5. Create a list of books that you'll read to stretch your thinking and develop the mind of Christ. Purchase or borrow one of the books on your list and set aside thirty minutes a day to dig into it. When you're finished, move right onto another one, maintaining the daily discipline of reading thirty minutes per day.

Phase 4

PERSEVERANCE

WEEK FOUR AND BEYOND

Practice 9

Challenge
Your Mind

FOCUS

determine to

be a lifelong

learner

Oftentimes, the most difficult part of a physical diet is simply making the decision to start, and then carrying out that start into a rhythm and pattern that produces results. But the next most difficult part is maintaining that rhythm and pattern day in, day out, for a lifetime. There are many temptations that lie along the path of health, often making it difficult to focus on the end goal of a healthy, energized lifestyle.

> A mind that is stretched by a new experience can never go back to its old dimensions.
> —Oliver Wendell Holmes

The same holds true for a mind renewal diet. It is a difficult process to begin, especially since most of us are accustomed to letting our minds run wherever they might. But *keeping* our minds healthy and active is an additional challenge that requires discipline and commitment.

So now that you've brought your thoughts into captivity, detoxified your mind, embarked on a new prayer life, sought accountability, acquired right thinking, and regulated your media intake, how can you maintain the momentum of those things? How can you forge a healthy lifestyle, living according to the principles outlined in this book?

The answer is practice nine: challenge your mind by committing to be a lifelong learner. With practice nine, you move into the fourth week of a three-week diet. In other words, you extend what you've learned and begin to apply it one day at a time for the rest of your life. You become a lifelong learner.

> If we're growing, we're always going to be outside our comfort zone.
> —John C. Maxwell

I have always attempted to be a learner. In fact, when I left college, I set a personal goal of being a lifelong learner. It is my belief that all leaders are learners. Bill Gates is a prime example. In an article by Evan Carmichael, Gates talked about the need for and benefits of lifelong learning.

"Every now and then I like to pick up a copy of *Time* magazine and read every article from beginning to end, not just the articles that interest me most," says Gates. "That way you can be certain to learn something you didn't know previously."

Many outsiders attribute Gates' success simply to his high level of intelligence. But for Gates, "Smart is an elusive concept." Instead, he attributes his success to his desire to never stop learning. "There's a certain sharpness, an ability to absorb new facts; to ask an insightful question; to relate two domains that may not seem connected at first." It is this curiosity that Gates tries to inspire in his workers, encouraging them to not only find answers but to ask the right questions.

For Gates, no matter what you spend your time doing in life, you should never stop asking questions; never stop learning. Whether you're an entrepreneur or a doctor or a software developer, it is only by increasing your understanding of the world around you that you will be able to have a significant impact. This is why Gates can still exclaim today, "I'm excited by the possibilities." If you never stop learning, you will never stop seeing the possibilities.[1]

Of course, being a lifelong learner doesn't necessarily mean you need to be familiar with the latest technology (an impossibility anyway) or cultural trends. Learning is such a broad topic that you'll need to personalize it.

ACTIVE LEARNING METHODS

In the most basic sense, we learn every day whether we want to or not. Our brains take in new information simply because there's new information all around us: a new pharmacy opens on the corner, a tree was struck by lightning last night, a left-turn light is added at the corner two blocks from your house. That type of learning is passive. This chapter, however, focuses on active learning. Active learning is when you are pursuing opportunities to increase your level of knowledge or experience.

It's important to know that active learning is not necessarily about going back to school and earning another degree. If your situation allows you to go back to school at this point in your life, that is a great opportunity. However, many people simply don't have that option. Maybe they have a preschooler at home or they're working two jobs or money is just too tight right now. In such situations, lifelong learning sounds more like a luxury than a possibility, let alone a necessity.

That's okay! The great news is you don't have to go to school to learn. You can be a lifetime learner right in the comfort of your very own home.

Here are a few methods that nearly anyone can use to pursue a lifetime of active learning outside the classroom.

> If you hold a cat by the tail, you learn things you cannot learn any other way.
>
> —Mark Twain

BOOKS

Never underestimate the value of a good book. It's been said that a person can become an expert on any topic simply by studying twelve to fifteen books in that field. Whether or not your goal is to become an expert, studying good books regularly is an out-standing way to challenge your mind and become a lifelong learner.

The key word, though, is study. Reading books is one thing, studying them is another. Studying involves applying the kind of higher thinking we discussed in the last chapter to your reading of books. Don't just let the words on the page flow through your mind and out the other side. Grab hold of them. Analyze and make connections. Evaluate and construct your own thoughts or opinions. That's when the real learning takes place.

> The purpose of learning is growth, and our minds, unlike our bodies, can continue growing as long as we live.
> —Mortimer Adler

Books are easier to come by in today's world than they have been before. Not only are mega-bookstores popping up in every city and town, you can also type a few words and numbers into your computer and have the precise book you're looking for delivered to your doorstep the next day. (Of course, in most cases you'll want to order them further ahead of time so that you don't have to pay for overnight shipping!) Or, although it might seem like an old-fashioned method, it still works and is remarkably inexpensive: visit your local library.

DISCUSSION GROUPS

One of the most helpful ways to process the information in a book is to discuss it in a group. In most any community, you'll find a group of people who either already are meeting to discuss books or would be very interested in doing so. You can join an existing group, or start your own, that is focused on the book or topic you most want to learn about.

For the LORD gives wisdom, and from his mouth come knowledge and understanding.

—Proverbs 2:6

The great value of a discussion group is that you can benefit from the thoughts, perspectives, and opinions of a group of people instead of just relying on your own insight. It's not cheating to learn from what others are thinking or the connections they're making between various thoughts and topics. Consider your discussion group a team. The goal is not for one individual to shine the brightest, but for the team as a whole to gain as much learning from the experience as possible.

But discussion groups don't have to be focused on a certain book or books. You could form a discussion group on any topic that interests you and a small group of people in your community—such as current events, leadership dynamics, or the theology of Calvin, Luther, or Arminius. In one sense, it's not even that important what topic you choose, except that it meets the standard of Philippians 4:8. You'll learn so much from the perspectives of others (and they'll learn from you) and you'll have plenty of opportunities to practice critical thinking and other higher thinking skills.

OTHER LEARNING OPPORTUNITIES

Keep your eyes open and you'll find plenty of opportunities to challenge your mind with lifetime learning.

If you're a parent of young children, check into the DK Eyewitness series of books. Your local library probably has them. They range in subject matter from cats to volcanoes and everything in between. The great thing about them is that they're laid out in short, informative paragraphs. You can read as much or as little as you want to in any session, and I promise that you'll learn something you didn't know!

Think about the people you know. Is your neighbor a master gardener? Ask her what she'd plant in your yard and why. Does someone in your small group take terrific pictures? Ask him what makes a great photo. Not only will you learn something, you'll strengthen your relationships as you show interest in what's important to others.

> Try to learn something about everything and everything about something.
> —Thomas Hardy

Watch a program on the History Channel, Discovery, National Geographic, PBS, or any of the educational channels that you might not typically view. Learn something about another country, another culture, or another time period.

Read a biography. You don't have to start with an eight-hundred-page book on George Washington. Consider a book from the children's or teen section of the library. Choose someone you know little about and read with anticipation.

Take an online class. There are hundreds of possibilities here and classes available for almost any subject you can imagine. Google *online class* to get started.

CHOOSING YOUR SPECIALIZATION

Practically speaking, it will be most beneficial to limit your efforts at lifetime learning to a handful of topics or areas at a time. There is so much information out there that, unless you focus, you might feel like you're drowning in it. To begin with, choose two or three specialty areas where you want to focus your learning. How do you choose from among so many options?

START WITH WHAT MOTIVATES YOU

If you don't enjoy cooking, you probably won't be extremely motivated to log on to www.allrecipes.com. If you're not all that interested in restoring classic cars, you're not likely to make the effort to visit the Barrett-Jackson car auction in Scottsdale, Arizona, every January. However, if reading Charles Spurgeon or Jonathan Edwards lights your fire, you'll remember to visit the Christian Classics Ethereal Library (www.ccel.org) fairly regularly. What are you passionate about? What really gets your blood pumping? What can you see yourself getting out of bed early on Saturday morning for? Mark down that spot. It might be a good choice as an area of study for your lifelong learning.

EXPAND YOUR INTERESTS

Maybe instead of choosing an area of study that you're already passionate about, you'll want to look beyond your usual interests and try to learn about a new topic. Maybe you've never tried reading one of the classic Christian writers or even thought you'd want to. But if you try to digest them in small doses at first (as mentioned in the previous chapter), you might find you really appreciate their depth and insight. So you'd rather order Mexican food than prepare it yourself, but what if you could duplicate your favorite green chili for a lot less than what it costs to eat out? Nobody's saying you have to read Luther's Bible commentaries cover to electronic cover or become a gourmet cook. But just by trying something new, you'll challenge your mind and improve your relationships with others since you'll have a new interest to discuss.

DECIDE WHETHER YOU WANT TO LEARN BROAD OR DEEP

One of my friends seems to be able to contribute to almost any conversation, not because he loves to hear himself talk, but because he has a broad base of knowledge across a wide range of subjects. He can talk about technology, music, sports, books, photography, great restaurants, and just about anything else because he's made it a point to explore new topics, new places, and a variety of subjects.

> The heart of the discerning acquires knowledge; the ears of the wise seek it out.
> —Proverbs 18:15

On the other hand, you may be a person who wants to know everything there is to know about Jack Russell terriers instead of just being able to talk about dogs in general. You want to know what their personalities are like, the perfect measurements and proportions, the most desirable colors, how easy they are to train, who the best breeders are, and so forth.

Personally, I like a combination of both approaches. I've determined to learn deep on certain subjects and broad on others. I want to know as much about God's Word as I possibly can, so I study it, ask God to help me understand it better, and read books about it so I can deepen my knowledge. Occasionally I enjoy playing a little golf and following the pros, but I don't play eighteen holes every week. My learning related to golf is broad rather than deep.

TAKE A MENTAL SURVEY

Look at the various areas of your life: spiritual, physical, mental, emotional. Now that you're well on your way with the renewing of your mind, can you identify a particular area you'd like to improve? Could your body use a little toning? Look into a new type of exercise. Do you struggle with anger? Maybe you need to work through a book that teaches you how to deal with this emotion. Learn for the sake of addressing a particular need or solving a problem.

APPLY WHAT YOU ALREADY KNOW

Remember our discussion about higher thinking? Learning isn't just about ingesting knowledge. It's about applying that knowledge to your circumstances, to your life. While there's something to be said for knowledge for its own sake, there's far more to be said for knowledge applied. In fact, some call wisdom applied knowledge. And the Bible says obtaining wisdom is to be a priority: "Choose my instruction instead of silver, knowledge rather than choice gold, for wisdom is more precious than rubies, and nothing you desire can compare with her" (Prov. 8:10–11).

THE HEART OF LEARNING

Really, it all comes down to a conscious decision on your part to live with a renewed mind day after day despite how you feel, just like living the life of a follower of Jesus. Jesus even said as much in Luke 9:23–25: "If anyone would come after me, he must deny himself and take up his cross daily and follow me. For whoever wants to save his life will lose it, but whoever loses his life for me will save it. What good is it for a man to gain the whole world, and yet lose or forfeit his very self?"

The answer couldn't be plainer. Living a mentally energetic, healthy life requires a daily commitment to self-denial. If we are to walk in the best mental capacity that God would have for us, we must deny ourselves both physically and mentally. We all have an inclination toward selfish desires that the Bible calls our sinful nature, a proclivity toward sin that is hardwired into us.

The apostle Paul discussed this at length in Romans 8. He wrote about our sinful nature and the magnificent way it is removed from us when we hand our hearts and minds over to the Creator. Take, for example, verses 5–10:

> Those who live according to the sinful nature have their minds set on what that nature desires; but those who live in accordance with the Spirit have their minds set on what the Spirit desires. The mind of sinful man is death,

but the mind controlled by the Spirit is life and peace; the sinful mind is hostile to God. It does not submit to God's law, nor can it do so. Those controlled by the sinful nature cannot please God.

You, however, are controlled not by the sinful nature but by the Spirit, if the Spirit of God lives in you. And if anyone does not have the Spirit of Christ, he does not belong to Christ. But if Christ is in you, your body is dead because of sin, yet your spirit is alive because of righteousness.

What does this mean to us? It means that we can live a life-long pattern of mental healthiness. Stop trying to live a mentally healthy life by your own strength and let God help you through it. Yes, temptations are going to arise, temptations to sin or just to let your new mental routine slack off a little more every day. But God has promised us that temptations don't have to get the best of us: "No temptation has seized you except what is common to man. And God is faithful; he will not let you be tempted beyond what you can bear. But when you are tempted, he will also provide a way out so that you can stand up under it" (1 Cor. 10:13).

These are the simple facts regarding a heart that has been turned over to the Creator. This is the type of lifestyle God wants you to have; it's the type of lifestyle he has provided to you. He has given you the opportunity to live this kind of life;

it's up to you to cooperate with the work that he wants to do in your life.

In Matthew 7:13–14, Jesus instructs us to "enter through the narrow gate. For wide is the gate and broad is the road that leads to destruction, and many enter through it. But small is the gate and narrow the road that leads to life, and only a few find it." The mind renewal diet may feel restrictive, but it is far from it. Our culture is continually telling us to travel the broad road, to walk through the wide gate, to make the easiest choice and put ourselves first. But that path only leads to destruction.

On the other hand, the narrow road, the small gate—these are the things that lead to life (John 10:10). And an abundant life at that! Are you tired, busy, or stressed out to the point where you are having trouble maintaining the purity of your thought life? Perhaps you're tired, busy, and stressed out *because* you haven't maintained the purity of your thought life! You've been walking the broad road and entering through the wide gate.

The good news is that God is faithful and will always be there when you need him. The narrow road is always a choice you can make. God is a constant, consistent God who is the same yesterday and today and forever (Heb. 13:8). As a loving Father, he delights in his children who turn their hearts toward him, regardless of what they've done in the past. If you get off track with your mind renewal diet, just remember that God wants to help you back on track and only needs you to desire it once more.

Encounter God in prayer. Look for him in the words of the Bible. Find him in your meetings with those who keep you accountable. Seek him out in his creation. He wants to be found. We only have to look for him on the narrow road.

LOCK IT DOWN

Now complete these five exercises to apply what you learned in this chapter.

1. Try Bill Gates' approach to reading a magazine. Read it cover to cover rather than picking and choosing which articles you read. What did you learn that you wouldn't have learned otherwise?

2. Journal your answers to the following questions: What most excites you about the possibility of being a lifelong learner? What reservations do you have? What do you think will be your biggest obstacles? Write a prayer that you can pray daily asking God to empower you to maintain a clean mind and a pure heart and to actively pursue a lifetime of learning.

3. Create a list of ten to fifteen topics that you think you might have some level of interest in learning about. Pray about your list for a day or two, and then begin to cut it down to

a short list of four to five topics. Once you have a short list, begin to investigate your possibilities for learning more about those topics through reading books, participating in groups or classes, and other opportunities. Begin your learning in one or two areas as soon as possible.

4. Create a plan for your first three months of lifelong learning. What will you study? How will you study it? How much time will you devote to it? What do you hope to learn? How do you expect your life will be different as a result of your learning? How will you share what you've learned with others? Write down as many specifics as you can so that you have a good, concrete plan.

5. Conduct a review of where you are and how far you've come in your thought life since you began reading *ReThink Your Life*. Have the results been what you've expected? Better? What do you think the reasons are? Then, review any principles or practices that you might have glossed over in your first reading of the book. Consider putting them into practice now. As you finish your review, thank God for his faithfulness and constant presence as you've worked this process.

What God Thinks about You

The following is a list of Bible verses that show how God thinks about you. These are helpful verses to read on a regular basis to keep your thoughts about yourself healthy.

- Genesis 1:27—"So God created man in his own image, in the image of God he created him; male and female he created them."

- Exodus 19:5—"Now if you obey me fully and keep my covenant, then out of all nations you will be my treasured possession."

- Deuteronomy 31:6—"The LORD your God goes with you; he will never leave you nor forsake you."

- Deuteronomy 33:12—"Let the beloved of the LORD rest secure in him, for he shields him all day long, and the one the LORD loves rests between his shoulders."

- Deuteronomy 33:27—"The eternal God is your refuge, and underneath are the everlasting arms."

- 2 Kings 17:39—"Worship the LORD your God; it is he who will deliver you from the hand of all your enemies."

- Psalm 5:12—"For surely, O LORD, you bless the righteous; you surround them with your favor as with a shield."

- Psalm 18:16–19—"He reached down from on high and took hold of me; he drew me out of deep waters. He rescued me from my powerful enemy, from my foes, who were too strong for me. They confronted me in the day of my disaster, but the LORD was my support. He brought me out into a spacious place; he rescued me because he delighted in me."

- Psalm 23:6—"Surely goodness and love will follow me all the days of my life, and I will dwell in the house of the LORD forever."

- Psalm 27:5—"For in the day of trouble he will keep me safe in his dwelling; he will hide me in the shelter of his tabernacle and set me high upon a rock."

- Psalm 32:7—"You are my hiding place; you will protect me from trouble and surround me with songs of deliverance."

- Psalm 48:14—"For this God is our God for ever and ever; he will be our guide even to the end."

- Psalm 91:11—"For he will command his angels concerning you to guard you in all your ways."

- Psalm 91:14–15—"'Because he loves me,' says the LORD, 'I will rescue him; I will protect him, for he acknowledges my name. He will call upon me, and I will answer him; I will be with him in trouble, I will deliver him and honor him.'"

- Psalm 100:3—"Know that the LORD is God. It is he who made us, and we are his; we are his people, the sheep of his pasture."

- Psalm 103:10–13—"He does not treat us as our sins deserve or repay us according to our iniquities. For as high as the heavens are above the earth, so great is his love for those who fear him; as far as the east is from the west, so far has he removed our transgressions from us. As a father has compassion on his children, so the LORD has compassion on those who fear him."

- Psalm 135:3–4—"Praise the LORD, for the LORD is good; sing praise to his name, for that is pleasant. For the LORD has chosen Jacob to be his own, Israel to be his treasured possession."

- Psalm 138:8—"The LORD will fulfill his purpose for me; your love, O LORD, endures forever."

- Psalm 139:1–4—"O LORD, you have searched me and you know me. You know when I sit and when I rise; you perceive my thoughts from afar. You discern my going out and my lying down; you are familiar with all my ways. Before a word is on my tongue you know it completely, O LORD."

- Psalm 145:9—"The LORD is good to all; he has compassion on all he has made."

- Psalm 145:13–14—"Your kingdom is an everlasting kingdom, and your dominion endures through all generations. The LORD is faithful to all his promises and loving toward all he has made. The LORD upholds all those who fall and lifts up all who are bowed down."

- Psalm 145:18–20—"The LORD is near to all who call on him, to all who call on him in truth. He fulfills the desires of those who fear him; he hears their cry and saves them. The LORD watches over all who love him."

- Psalm 147:11—"The LORD delights in those who fear him, who put their hope in his unfailing love."

- Isaiah 41:13—"For I am the LORD, your God, who takes hold of your right hand and says to you, Do not fear; I will help you."

- Isaiah 43:4—"You are precious and honored in my sight, and . . . I love you."

- Isaiah 44:22—"I have swept away your offenses like a cloud, your sins like the morning mist. Return to me, for I have redeemed you."

- Isaiah 46:4—"Even to your old age and gray hairs I am he, I am he who will sustain you. I have made you and I will carry you; I will sustain you and I will rescue you."

- Isaiah 48:17—"This is what the LORD says—your Redeemer, the Holy One of Israel: 'I am the LORD your God, who teaches you what is best for you, who directs you in the way you should go.'"

- Isaiah 49:16—"See, I have engraved you on the palms of my hands."

- Isaiah 54:10—"'Though the mountains be shaken and the hills be removed, yet my unfailing love for you will not be shaken nor my covenant of peace be removed,' says the LORD, who has compassion on you."

- Isaiah 58:11—"The LORD will guide you always; he will satisfy your needs in a sun-scorched land and will strengthen your frame. You will be like a well-watered garden, like a spring whose waters never fail."

- Jeremiah 1:5—"Before I formed you in the womb I knew you, before you were born I set you apart."

- Jeremiah 29:11—"'For I know the plans I have for you,' declares the LORD, 'plans to prosper you and not to harm you, plans to give you hope and a future.'"

- Jeremiah 31:3—"The LORD appeared to us in the past, saying: 'I have loved you with an everlasting love; I have drawn you with loving-kindness.'"

- Jeremiah 32:40—"I will make an everlasting covenant with them: I will never stop doing good to them, and I will inspire them to fear me, so that they will never turn away from me."

- Ezekiel 34:12, 31—"As a shepherd looks after his scattered flock when he is with them, so will I look after my sheep. I will rescue them from all the places where they were scattered on a day of clouds and darkness. . . . You my sheep, the sheep of my pasture, are people, and I am your God, declares the Sovereign LORD."

- Hosea 2:19—"I will betroth you to me forever; I will betroth you in righteousness and justice, in love and compassion."

- Zephaniah 3:17—"The LORD your God is with you, he is mighty to save. He will take great delight in you, he will quiet you with his love, he will rejoice over you with singing."

- Matthew 7:11—"If you, then, though you are evil, know how to give good gifts to your children, how much more will your Father in heaven give good gifts to those who ask him!"

- John 1:12—"Yet to all who received him, to those who believed in his name, he gave the right to become children of God."

- John 8:36—"So if the Son sets you free, you will be free indeed."

- John 14:2–3 — "In my Father's house are many rooms; if it were not so, I would have told you. I am going there to prepare a place for you. And if I go and prepare a place for you, I will come back and take you to be with me that you also may be where I am."

- John 15:16 — "You did not choose me, but I chose you and appointed you to go and bear fruit — fruit that will last. Then the Father will give you whatever you ask in my name."

- John 17:23 — "I in them and you in me. May they be brought to complete unity to let the world know that you sent me and have loved them even as you have loved me."

- Acts 17:28 — "'For in him we live and move and have our being.' As some of your own poets have said, 'We are his offspring.'"

- Romans 5:8 — "But God demonstrates his own love for us in this: While we were still sinners, Christ died for us."

- Romans 8:31 — "What, then, shall we say in response to this? If God is for us, who can be against us?"

- Romans 8:35, 37–39 — "Who shall separate us from the love of Christ? Shall trouble or hardship or persecution or famine or nakedness or danger or sword? . . . No, in all these things we are more than conquerors through him who loved us. For I am convinced that neither death nor life, neither angels nor demons, neither the present nor the future, nor any powers, neither height nor depth, nor anything else in all creation, will be able to separate us from the love of God that is in Christ Jesus our Lord."

- 2 Corinthians 6:18 — "I will be a Father to you, and you will be my sons and daughters, says the Lord Almighty."

- Ephesians 1:4–8 — "For he chose us in him before the creation of the world to be holy and blameless in his sight. In love he predestined us to be adopted as his sons through Jesus Christ, in accordance with his pleasure and will — to the praise of his glorious grace, which he has freely given us in the One he loves. In him we have redemption through his blood, the forgiveness of sins, in accordance with the riches of God's grace that he lavished on us with all wisdom and understanding."

- Ephesians 1:11–12 — "In him we were also chosen, having been predestined according to the plan of him who works out everything in conformity with the purpose of his will, in order that we, who were the first to hope in Christ, might be for the praise of his glory."

- Ephesians 5:25–27—"Christ loved the church and gave himself up for her to make her holy, cleansing her by the washing with water through the word, and to present her to himself as a radiant church, without stain or wrinkle or any other blemish, but holy and blameless."

- 2 Thessalonians 2:16–17—"May our Lord Jesus Christ himself and God our Father, who loved us and by his grace gave us eternal encouragement and good hope, encourage your hearts and strengthen you in every good deed and word."

- 2 Timothy 1:9—"Who has saved us and called us to a holy life—not because of anything we have done but because of his own purpose and grace. This grace was given us in Christ Jesus before the beginning of time."

- 1 Peter 2:9—"You are a chosen people, a royal priesthood, a holy nation, a people belonging to God, that you may declare the praises of him who called you out of darkness into his wonderful light."

- 1 John 3:1—"How great is the love the Father has lavished on us, that we should be called children of God! And that is what we are!"

- 1 John 4:10—"This is love: not that we loved God, but that he loved us and sent his Son as an atoning sacrifice for our sins."

Appendix B

Selected Media Resources that Promote Healthy Thoughts

This appendix provides lists of recommended media that will help you as you strive to incorporate higher thinking into your life. The lists are by no means comprehensive, but rather a few suggestions that I hope will serve as a launching pad to a lifetime pursuit of higher thinking. And though I recommend this media, I cannot completely guarantee your experience with it. Styles and tastes differ. These are merely my humble recommendations.

BOOKS

Celebration of Discipline, Richard J. Foster

Chronicles of Narnia, The, C. S. Lewis

Divine Conspiracy, The, Dallas Willard

Enjoying the Presence of God, Jan Johnson

Fear and Trembling, Søren Kierkegaard

Fresh Wind, Fresh Fire, Jim Cymbala

How Should We Then Live? Francis Schaeffer

Imitation of Christ, Thomas à Kempis

Jesus I Never Knew, The, Philip Yancey

Mere Christianity, C. S. Lewis

My Utmost for His Highest, Oswald Chambers

Peace Like a River, Leif Enger

Pilgrim's Progress, The, John Bunyan

Power of Positive Praying, The, John Bisagno

Practicing the Presence of God, Brother Lawrence

Praying Psalm 23, Elmer L. Towns

Real Christianity, William Wilberforce

Renovation of the Heart, Dallas Willard

Screwtape Letters, The, C. S. Lewis

Severe Mercy, A, Sheldon Vanauken

Spiritual Leadership, J. Oswald Sanders

Traveling Mercies, Anne Lamott

What's So Amazing about Grace? Philip Yancey

MAGAZINES AND NEWSPAPERS

Biblical Archaeology Review

Christianity Today

Discipleship Journal

Newsweek

Rev!

Time

Wall Street Journal

Washington Post

MOVIES

12 Angry Men

African Queen, The

Amazing Grace

Apollo 13

Babe

Bicycle Thief, The

Bugs Life, A

Casablanca

Chariots of Fire

Citizen Kane

Count of Monte Cristo, The

Dead Poets Society

End of the Spear

Fiddler on the Roof

Field of Dreams

Finding Nemo

Finding Neverland

Forever Young

Hook

Hoosiers

Hotel Rwanda

Incredibles, The

It's a Wonderful Life

Lawrence of Arabia

Life Is Beautiful

Lion, the Witch, and the Wardrobe, The

Little Princess, The

Lord of the Rings, The

Man in the Iron Mask, The

Man Without a Face, The

Mr. Holland's Opus

My Fair Lady

Operation Dumbo Drop

Passion of the Christ, The

Rudy

Schindler's List

Seabiscuit

Secondhand Lions

Secret Garden, The

Sound of Music, The

To Kill a Mockingbird

Toy Story

MUSIC

Lifesong, Casting Crowns

Duets, Tony Bennett

Genius Loves Company, Ray Charles

Kind of Blue, Miles Davis

Live, Michael Bublé

Lovin' Life, Gaither Vocal Band

One Flight Down, Norah Jones

Unforgettable, Natalie Cole

Wow! Worship series

WEB SITES

http://apod.nasa.gov/apod

> This is NASA's Astronomy Picture of the Day Web site, and it is awesome!

http://news.google.com

http://www.beliefnet.com/index/index_10002.html

http://www.biblegateway.com

http://www.brecksong.com

http://www.cybersalt.org/cleanlaugh

http://www.dictionary.com

> You can sign up for a word of the day e-mail and thereby broaden your vocabulary.

http://www.iequip.org

http://www.leaderlinks.com

http://www.maximumimpact.com

http://www.snopes.com

> The urban legends debunking page—this one's great for stopping dumb e-mail forwards.

http://www.stantoler.com

http://www.tolerleadershipcenter.com

http://www.wikipedia.org

Media Inventory Worksheet

On the next page, you'll find a worksheet you can use to complete a personal media inventory. You have permission to make photocopies of the worksheet for personal use.

INSTRUCTIONS

Write today's date in the blank provided, then list each media item you consumed today, how you consumed it (TV, radio, Internet, etc.), for how long, for what purpose, and your evaluation of whether the item filled your mind with mostly healthy thoughts, unhealthy thoughts, or mixed.

MEDIA INVENTORY WORKSHEET

Inventory Date: _____

What?	How?	How long?	Why?	Evaluation

Permission granted to photocopy this worksheet for personal use.

Media Meal Plan Worksheet

O n the next page, you'll find a worksheet to help you create a media meal plan. You may photocopy the worksheet for personal use.

INSTRUCTIONS

List all the types of media that you plan to use in the coming week, along with how much time you think it will take and any potential dangers you see in consuming that particular item.

MEDIA MEAL PLAN WORKSHEET

Type of Media	Titles	Projected Time	Potential Dangers
TV Shows			
Movies or DVD's			
Music			
Books			
Magazines			
Newspapers			
Web Sites			
E-mail			

Permission granted to photocopy this worksheet for personal use.

Sample Accountability Covenant

We covenant together, as brothers or sisters in Christ, to meet at least twice a month for the purpose of holding one another accountable in our efforts to maintain pure hearts and clean minds. We further agree to continue meeting in this way over the course of the next six months.

We agree that the content of our meetings will remain confidential. We will not disclose the thoughts expressed by or emotions observed in another person at our meetings without the specific permission of the person. This includes both public disclosure (prayer requests, sermon illustrations, blogging) as well as private disclosure (conversations with friends, coworkers, family members, or friends). Details about conversations or interactions are not to be shared without permission even if you change the name or otherwise mask the identity of the other person.

We agree that the purpose of our meeting together is not to counsel, mentor, or supervise one another, but to provide Christian support and accountability. We will do so, not with harsh words and critical judgment, but with compassionate listening, encouraging words, and assertive, straightforward communication.

Agreed in Christ:

Name: _____

Name: _____

Name: _____

Date: _____

Accountability
Questions

U se these questions to dig more deeply as you share in accountability meetings. You certainly don't need to use every one every time, but, as mentioned in the text, the last question in every session should be "Have you answered all of these questions truthfully?"

For more instruction on how to use the questions or what to do in an accountability meeting, see Practice 6: Create a Circle of Accountability.

1. How have you done with maintaining your integrity this week? What have you done that might have compromised your integrity?

2. What did you do this week to make progress in accomplishing your spiritual goals? What challenges have you faced in pursuing your spiritual goals this week?

3. How much and what kinds of media did you consume this week? Describe what the content of your media intake has been like. Describe any changes you'd like to make in your media intake before our next meeting.

4. How are you doing with prioritizing people over media right now? Where might you be struggling with that?

5. How are you doing with taking every thought captive? What kinds of thoughts have been continually popping up in your mind? What kinds of thoughts have surprised you? What have you done with those thoughts?

6. How much have you let your mind wander this week? Where has it wandered to? What did you do to rein it in?

7. What kinds of healthy thoughts are you trying to focus on right now? How is that going for you?

8. What do you want me to pray with you about this week?

9. What are you struggling with most right now? Where are you having the most victory right now?

10. How are you feeling about our accountability partnership today? Are there ways we can make it more beneficial for you?

11. Have you answered all of my questions truthfully?

Appendix G

Bloom's Taxonomy

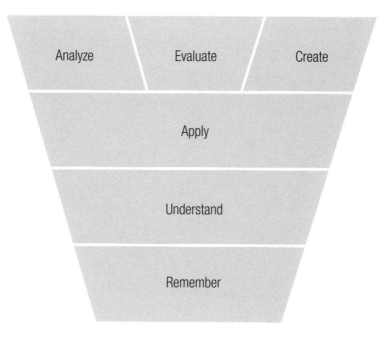

| Analyze | Evaluate | Create |
| Apply |
| Understand |
| Remember |

Source: http://commons.wikimedia.org/wiki/Image:BloomsCognitiveDomain.PNG

Notes

INTRODUCTION

1. Stan Toler, *Total Quality Life: Strategies for Purposeful Living* (Indianapolis: Wesleyan Publishing House, 2007), 39.

PRACTICE 1

1. C. S. Lewis, *Mere Christianity* (New York: Macmillan, 1966), 86.

2. Marketdata Enterprises, Inc., Full Industry Studies, http://www.mkt-data-ent.com/studies.html (accessed Feb. 7, 2008).

3. United States Department of Agriculture, "Inside the Pyramid," http://www.mypyramid.gov/pyramid/index.html (accessed May 22, 2008).

PRACTICE 2

1. Laurence O'Donnell, "Music and the Brain," http://www.cerebro-mente.org.br/n15/mente/musica.html (accessed Feb. 14, 2008).

2. Media Awareness Network, "Research on the Effects of Media Violence," http://www.media-awareness.ca/english/issues/violence/effects_media_violence.cfm (accessed Feb. 14, 2008).

3. Mercola.com, "How Television Affects Your Brain Chemistry" (video clip), http://articles.mercola.com/sites/articles/archive/2007/10/20/how-television-affects-your-brain-chemistry-and-that-s-not-all.aspx (accessed Feb. 13, 2008).

4. Wikipedia, "Information overload," http://en.wikipedia.org/wiki/Information_overload (accessed Feb. 14, 2008).

5. Bridget Murray, "Data Smog: Newest Culprit in Brain Drain," APA Online, http://www.apa.org/monitor/mar98/smog.html (accessed Feb. 14, 2008).

PRACTICE 3

1. Neil T. Anderson, *Victory Over the Darkness* (Ventura: Gospel Light, 1994).

PRACTICE 4

1. James F. Strange, "Sepphoris," The Bible and Interpretation, http://www.bibleinterp.com/articles/sepphoris.htm (accessed May 23, 2008).

2. Barbara F. McManus, "Leisure and Entertainment," http://www.vroma.org/~bmcmanus/leisure.html (accessed Feb. 16, 2008).

3. History Learning Site, "Roman Entertainment,"
http://www.historylearningsite.co.uk/roman_entertainment.htm
(accessed Feb. 16, 2008).

PRACTICE 5

1. Leonard Sweet, *11* (Colorado Springs: David C. Cook, 2008), 98–99.

PRACTICE 6

1. Mars Hill, "Prayer of Examen,"
http://www.marshill.org/advent/examen.php (accessed May 23, 2008)

2. Rob Jackson, "Foundations for Life: How to Develop Effective Accountability," Focus on the Family,
http://www.pureintimacy.org/gr/intimacy/redemption/a0000151.cfm
(accessed May 23, 2008).

PRACTICE 8

1. Adapted from Lynn Schultz, "Bloom's Taxonomy,"
http://www.odu.edu/educ/roverbau/bloom/blooms_taxonomy.htm
(accessed May 23, 2008).

PRACTICE 9

1. Evan Carmichael, "Lesson #5: Never Stop Learning,"
http://www.evancarmichael.com/Famous-Entrepreneurs/556/Lesson-5-Never-Stop-Learning.html (accessed Feb. 21, 2008).

About the Author

S tan Toler is executive director of the Toler Leadership Center located on the campus of Mid-America Christian University and is an internationally recognized authority on leadership and personal development. He also serves as senior pastor at Trinity Church of the Nazarene in Oklahoma City. For several years he taught with Dr. John Maxwell's INJOY Group, a leadership development institute. Toler has written more than seventy books including these best-sellers—

God Has Never Failed Me, But He's Sure
Scared Me to Death a Few Times

The Buzzards Are Circling, But God's Not Finished with Me Yet

God's Never Late, He's Seldom Early, He's Always Right on Time

The Secret Blend

Practical Guide to Pastoral Ministry

Total Quality Life

Minute Motivator series

For additional information on seminars, scheduling speaking engagements, or to contact the author:

STAN TOLER
PO Box 892170
Oklahoma City, OK 73189-2170
E-mail: stoler1107@aol.com
Web site: www.StanToler.com

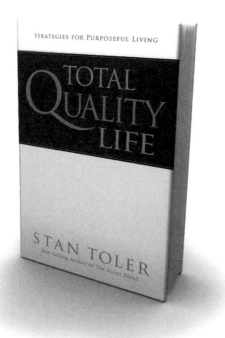

STRATEGIES FOR PURPOSEFUL LIVING

TOTAL
QUALITY
LIFE

STAN TOLER
Best-Selling Author of *The Secret Blend*

Also By Stan Toler

Total Quality Life: Strategies for Purposeful Living
is a practical guidebook to help you take charge of your personal,
professional, and spiritual life, empowering you to live
with purpose, effectiveness, and significance.

ISBN: 978-0-89827-360-1
www.wesleyan.org/wph